STALEFISH

STALEFISH

Skateboard Culture from
the Rejects Who Made It

By Sean Mortimer
Foreword by Tony Hawk

CHRONICLE BOOKS
SAN FRANCISCO

Cover Todd Swank. **Photo:** Grant Brittain

P. 1 (Clockwise from top left)

Chris Haslam, spotting skate spots where most don't, L.A. County, 2006. **Photo:** Courtesy of Dwindle Dist.

Tommy Guerrero, Santa Monica, 1987. **Photo:** Grant Brittain

Christian Hosoi, Capitola, 1984. **Photo:** Grant Brittain

P. 2 (Clockwise from top left)

Mike Vallely, Carson, contest, 1987. **Photo:** Sean Mortimer

Tony Hawk, frontside air 24-foot gap, desert, 2001. **Photo:** Grant Brittain

Product Toss, Capitola, 1984. **Photo:** Grant Brittain

PP. 4–5 Bones Brigade Demo. Carlsbad, 1986. **Photo:** Grant Brittain

DEDICATION

For Tony, Kevin, Rodney, and Lance, who showed me that skateboarding is more than just skateboarding. And Coop, Ronin, and Francesca, of course.

Library of Congress Cataloging-in-Publication Data available.

ISBN: 978-0-8118-6042-0

Manufactured in China

Designed by Scott Thorpe

Headline Typeface by Brett MacFadden
(Inspired by the Powell Peralta Tony Hawk decks of 1983–1987)

10 9 8 7 6 5 4 3 2 1

Chronicle Books LLC
680 Second Street
San Francisco, California 94107
www.chroniclebooks.com

CONTENTS

1

By Tony Hawk

Skateboarding is a lifestyle, an art form, a sport, a career, an escape from responsibility, a hobby, a mode of transport, a kids' pastime, a form of rebellion, a booming industry, a form of expression, family entertainment, a genre of video games, a healthy form of exercise, a dangerous activity, an addiction, a culture, an identity, an education, and even a religion to faithful followers. How is it possible that a plank of wood, two pieces of metal, and four urethane wheels bolted together can represent so much to people? I can only speak for myself, but I was hooked the moment I stepped on one at the age of nine. It felt free, liberating, boundless. I didn't have to rely on a team for my own success, nor did I have to adhere to a strict set of rules to play correctly. I could do it in my own style, on my own terms, and still be accepted in this exciting new world.

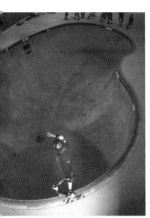

2

3

4

Along with my new passion, I found a new group of friends. People from many different backgrounds that never quite "fit in" to their respective communities found a common bond by simply skating together. I had an extended family of outcasts and misfits at the skatepark so I ended up spending all of my free time there.

There are so many personalities that helped shape skateboarding in these formative years that it's impossible to generalize the average skater. Instead, Sean decided to find the main pioneers and get their stories. This was no easy task; many of the legendary skaters are aloof and don't necessarily want to share their backgrounds. But Sean persevered and managed to painstakingly track them down—verging on stalking at times—in order for us to understand the obsession that consumed most of their lives.

As much as I am part of this story, I am equally a fan of the other stars. Their pictures were plastered all over my walls, their names were synonymous with revolutionary tricks, and I wanted to emulate them however I could. Their stories are all fascinating in their devotion and sanctity. I am glad to read their insights and experiences to find that we are all kindred spirits, still enjoying what we love as we get older.

This book will give you a better understanding of where skateboarding came from, how it evolved, and where it is headed. These are the characters that have shaped it and the ones that continue its progression. Embrace the history and enjoy the future.

INTRODUCTION: INVASION OF THE DESK PEOPLE

Steve Olson, carve grind, Hester series, 1978. Photo: James Cassimus

Chris Haslam, definitely not thinking of sweeping, former meth lab. 2006. Photo: Courtesy of Dwindle Dist.

1
2

This isn't a history book—no carbon-dating the first lapper here. Okay, some historic dates are included, like the time Steve Olson picked his nose onstage as his 1978 Skater of the Year speech. Besides documenting that significant incident, there were two motivations behind *Stalefish*.

1. Answer the icky question that has stuck to skateboarding like gum on a sneaker: Is it a sport?

2. Celebrate the culture that grew from collecting scabs on a toy designed for children while getting chased out of play areas.

At first, I had no idea how to address these two points, but I had watched enough characters "explain" skateboarding in corny movies like

1

2

Gleaming the Cube to be very afraid. Lance Mountain voices a similar warning: "There's always a bit of defining what a 'real' skateboarder is from companies …[and] it's never what anybody behind a desk is telling you." I didn't want to be one of those gross desk people.

But I did want to show how skating can derail your life in a beautiful way, unlike traditional sports. Tommy Guerrero half-jokingly refers to it as a cult, and I think most core skaters would agree. That's why it can sting when a network of behind-the-deskers broadcast their version of skateboarding to the general population. The proliferation and apparent success of these televised skate events, mostly created by nonskaters who have manipulated them into easily recognized jock templates, lit the fuse for this book. Emphasizing the competitive aspect, which can matter squat inside the skateboard world, and ignoring the cultural influence sucks and spits out the most significant aspect of skating. This culture that has been molded by rejection, creativity, and a bunch of

other fun stuff runs so deep that most skaters visibly recoil when referred to as "athletes."

But some skaters, like Russ Howell, embrace that label. And others have violently reversed their opinion over the years. Skating's short and chaotic history often produces clashing views, and *Stalefish* throws together interviews from influential devotees who span the time-line of skating. Their varied experiences reflect the reactionary culture of skate-boarding while proving that the nucleus, the unifying reason why we all skate, holds strong fifty years after kids were first yelled at for making a racket on amputated apple-crate scooters. Their experiences answer the uncomfortable "sport" question by celebrating the reject culture of skating.

Or maybe it's just a gang of scab collectors yapping. Whatever this book is, hopefully it will make you want to grip it and rip it.

TIMELINE

1975

Del Mar hosts a "surfer stomp" and a chaotic skateboard contest. A legendary battle is waged between edgier surf-style skateboarding and ballet-, ice skating–, and gymnastics-influenced riding. Dirtbag surf rats lose the contest but win the war. (And, decades later, make a movie about it.)

1978

Skate superstar Tony Alva stars in the Leif Garrett flick *Skateboard: the Movie*, rocking massive radio headphones secured with a bandana. He farts in the bus scene.

1979

Stacy Peralta saves a European crown prince from assassination on *Charlie's Angels*.

1980

Skateboarding wakes up dead. There are approximately twenty-seven skaters left rolling around the world—sort of like a skateboarding Rapture, after which only hardcore rejects are left on earth. *SkateBoarder*, widely considered the "bible" by enthusiasts, reinvents itself as *Action Now*, mixing together BMX, sandboarding, and equestrian weirdness. It receives no action.

1985

Skateboarding's popularity grows in a subterranean direction. Lance Mountain lights his board on fire for his final "Terror in Tahoe" contest run. A dead cat is pitched through the air in the ensuing celebration.

1992

What happened? A strange plague affects skaters, and virtually all quit. The largest skateboard companies crumble, and free-style skateboarding is killed dead. No major company ever produces freestyle product again.

1995

The Extreme Olympics are created by ESPN, lumping skateboarding in with professional bungee jumping. The street course is painted questionable colors. Nonskating announcers report that competitors are judged on their "amplitude," whatever that is.

1998

Skating is enjoying increased popularity just as Satan finally arrives on earth. He takes the form of Chris Loarie and invents Skatestoppers, which are renamed "Nazi knobs" by skaters. Skaters employ their high-school shop educations, using blowtorches, hacksaws, and crowbars to remove them.

1957

First recorded account of skate harassment: Jim Fitzpatrick's grandma yells at him for riding a skateboard outside her house.

1965

Skateboarding is rad! It's on the cover of *Life*. Future world champion Russ Howell bikes twenty miles to see the first national skateboard contest in Anaheim, gets lost in an orange orchard, and misses the historic event.

1967

Skateboarding is dangerous! And not much fun on metal or clay wheels. The fad is dead.

1973

Frank Nasworthy makes skateboard wheels out of urethane and the increased speed, traction, and control resurrect the fad. It's official: Skateboarding is fun again.

1981

Thrasher magazine hits the street. The issues are made of old-school newsprint that blackens your fingers with ink and captures the DIY feeling of skating at the time.

1982

Mark Gonzales, Natas Kaupas, and Tommy Guerrero adapt the best aspects of freestyle and vert to the streets. Most freestyle and vert skaters laugh and openly question whether street style is even a legitimate style of skating. Laughter turns to tears years later, when street becomes the dominant form of skating.

1983

Wait a sec, *Thrasher*. *Transworld Skateboarding* magazine offers its version of skating with a glossy magazine that won't dirty the digits.

1984

Over coffee on a lazy Sunday afternoon, Rodney Mullen and Tony Hawk agree to dominate vert and freestyle contests for a decade or so. Rodney informs Tony that he already started four years ago. Powell Peralta releases the first skateboard video, detonating the most powerful form of marketing in skateboarding.

1999

Tony Hawk lands the 900 on international TV and unleashes a curse on himself. Whenever he does a demo afterward, people scream for one of the most difficult tricks ever landed. He also releases a best-selling video-game series. Nonskating gamers can now comfortably use "stalefish" and "sacktap" in a sentence.

2001

Stacy Peralta directs *Dogtown and Z-Boys*. The award-winning documentary explores the impact of the 1970s-era Zephyr shop-sponsored skate rats. Ignorant younger skaters finally appreciate and understand their past. Old dudes start riding again and paying thousands for collectible old-school decks that had been worthless six months earlier.

2003

The skateboard movie *Grind* is released, continuing the long tradition of mainstream-cheese skateboard cinema. (*Thrashin'* and *Gleaming the Cube* remain the standard, though.)

2007

During the X Games, Jake Brown falls off his skateboard from approximately forty-five feet above the mega-ramp flat, and blows his shoes off upon impact. He walks away with assistance. Finally, after years of watching mainstream televised skate events, the armchair fans get to see what they really wanted—a worthy slam. See? Skateboarding is dangerous. And Jake rules.

IN NO WAY AM I CROWNING THE SIXTEEN SKATERS INTERVIEWED IN THIS BOOK THE "BEST" SKATERS. But they are some of the most highly regarded shredders and have been pivotal participants in the shaping of skateboarding. Of course, there are other skaters who fit in this group, but these riders embody different aspects of our culture, and I avoided, as much as possible, talking to people who shared a lot of similar experiences. All the skaters here are famous professionals who directly shaped the scene, but their love for skating is no different from that of kids who shred their shins attempting kickflips, or of Red and his friends, who built Burnside skatepark under a scummy Oregon bridge with no fanfare.

Makaha reportedly sold a staggering $4 million worth of skateboards from 1963 to 1965, and little **Jim Fitzpatrick**, the first on its team, rode the company's newfangled product in Southern California parks and grocery-store openings to introduce skating to the masses.

Fitz, now sixty, still skateboards in his downtime from duties at the Montessori school in Santa Barbara where he reigns as principal. Previously, he worked at Powell Peralta, and he is currently the vice president of USA Skateboarding. "I never paid for a skateboard until 1999," he said, "when a kid stole my longboard from outside my classroom. I had to buy it back from the neighbor for $20."

Jim Fitzpatrick, Brentwood, 1964. **Photo:** Courtesy of Jim Fitzpatrick

JF: In the summer of 1957, I was nine years old and living in San Diego. One day a bunch of us were driving our neighbor, an engineer who also worked on Jaguars and high-end bicycles in his garage, nuts. To distract us, Mr. Wilson showed us how to make skate scooters using two-by-fours and roller-skate parts. But since we didn't attach an apple crate to the wheels, somebody called them skateboards.

These weren't built to last, very impermanent—we just used nails to keep the trucks on. They all looked different, because we'd used whatever scrap wood was around and all had different-length boards.

It was just this new thing, and we didn't even know what to do with it. Mr. Wilson had to show us how to stand on it, because he knew from riding apple-crate scooters as a kid. You couldn't really adjust the trucks and turn, so you could only skate in a straight line. We'd point the board and go until we had to jump off and bail. It was simple, but they were so dangerous that there was a thrill and excitement to just riding across the street. Every twig, the smallest pebble—anything—derailed you instantly.

We were a pack of five and then ten skateboarders, and the noise was horrific with the steel wheels—metal on cement, a sort of grinding. Sometimes I'd get vibrated off my board. My first experience of skate harassment was my grandma yelling at me from her front porch to stop it.

I figured a two-by-four was the wrong piece of wood for a skateboard. I experimented with different sizes of wood and used roofing tacks instead of nails on thinner wood. But they vibrated out, and my truck would fall off. My dad finally asked me why I wasn't using screws.

But riding these things was just a summer-vacation experience. We'd burn out on them after a certain point. I moved to Malibu in 1960, when I was twelve, and met two guys who made skateboards based on mine. I know now that Roller Derby skateboards were in stores in 1959, but I never saw one.

In 1962, Bill Cleary, one of the surfers I knew, began working as an editor for *Surf Guide*. Its founder, Larry Stevenson, used the magazine to market the skateboards he was developing. Cleary gave me a prototype of the early Makaha, and it was like going from a bicycle to a car. Stevenson's early Makaha prototype used *indoor* clay wheels; Roller Derby had been making clay wheels earlier, but nobody had had the wherewithal to look at indoor skate wheels instead of metal ones. Actually, they weren't really pure clay. They were an early composite. Stevenson was taking these wheels and a rudimentary truck and attaching them to oak planks shaped like surfboards. You could turn—the wheels were a lot more forgiving and a little farther apart, so you had stability. The rear truck was not mounted on the tail, and you could tic-tac or kickturn for the first time. There was also added danger—we were suddenly going two to three times faster.

By the end of 1962, they were manufacturing Makaha boards, the first modern skateboards, and advertising them in the magazine. They used surf icons Mike Doyle and Mike Hynson. Stevenson figured that if he could get the surf crowd to sidewalk-surf, he had a built-in market. But I never saw older skaters—no twenty-five-year-old ever pushed me off my board and took it. Stevenson would send me to downtown Santa Monica just to ride in public. He'd drop me off at Lincoln Park, and my job was to skate around, do some tic tacs, skate in a circle, and create this furor with the kids.

BUT I NEVER SAW OLDER SKATERS—NO TWENTY-FIVE-YEAR-OLD EVER PUSHED ME OFF MY BOARD AND TOOK IT.

By 1964 we had a Makaha skateboard team. Jim Ganzer, who later started Jimmy'Z, was our team manager. I was fourteen and he was eighteen. It took around three years from when they started giving me boards to organizing a skateboard team. Of course, we didn't consider ourselves pro or sponsored, we were just "on the team."

That same year, Hobie started making skateboards, and he sold a lot of skateboards in the San Diego area, whereas Makaha was the local company in the L.A. area. There were very few retailers, and the distribution was mostly through surf shops and surfing-magazine mail-order. But even then, if you went into a surf shop in 1964, there wasn't anything for sale. There was no surf wax, and they didn't sell T-shirts—nothing existed to be bought, because

you had to make it on your own. A surf shop was basically a place to get a custom board shaped.

In the summer of '65, I graduated from high school. By then I was going out with girls, and skateboarding took a backseat. I got a job, bought a car, and started working in Hollywood and going to college.

A skate mag once christened **Russ Howell** "Russ the Brush" for his "magnificent mustache." The Brush, who was often a decade older than his teenage competitors, began collecting trophies after winning the 1975 Del Mar freestyle contest. His string of wins and mainstream endorsement deals made him what many insiders considered the first professional skateboarder.

Russ's mature perspective, his bachelor's degree in physical education, and his promotion of skateboarding as a sport clashed with the attitudes of the disenfranchised majority. He proves that skating isn't an easily categorized activity that can be pushed into an existing slot. Russ continues to skate with passion, even just shy of sixty. Up until a few years ago, he had a ramp in his Boise, Idaho, backyard, and he can still kick ass spinning 360s: "I'm still skating freestyle, and I can still spin eighty 360s, which isn't much for me."

Russ Howell, multideck handstand, Free Former contest, 1976. **Photo:** James Cassimus

RH: Back in 1958, when I first started skating, it was called surfing's little brother. In fifth grade, we'd roll down sidewalks on our Roller Derby skateboards and play on the blacktop playgrounds, and if you hit a rock, you were dead. Skateboarding became the craze in Southern California.

My friends and I skimboarded, surfed, skated—it was just part of the California social atmosphere. I never attended the sock-hop dances in junior high and high school, just stayed outside and danced on my skateboard. People came out and watched.

In the mid-'60s, there was a Jack's skateboard team and a Hobie team. My friends and I learned really quick that most skateboards were made as toys, so we'd shape our own decks using oak from the lumberyard.

I NEVER ATTENDED THE SOCK-HOP DANCES IN JUNIOR HIGH AND HIGH SCHOOL, JUST STAYED OUTSIDE AND DANCED ON MY SKATEBOARD.

Skateboarding was in its infancy and looking for something to cling to—in what direction were you going to push this sport, what can you do with it? Obviously, you looked at other sports. Being surfers, we walked the board,

hung ten, did nose wheelies—the Quasimodo and coffin. The gymnastic influence came in with snow skiing. Snow skiing had freestyle and slalom, and surfing was pretty much all freestyle, so we tried to integrate it all and see what we could do on a skateboard. At that time, I learned handstands on park benches, and taking it to the skateboard was a natural progression. Out of all this came freestyle footwork, handstands, inverted tricks, multiple board tricks, spins, and aerial tricks.

My first contest was a Huntington Beach city championship in 1975, when I was twenty-five, and I won in freestyle. My next contest was the 1975 Nationals, the Ocean Festival in Del Mar that the *Dogtown* movie popularized. While attending Cal State Long Beach, I was teaching a group of young kids how to skate at a local park. One of the kids came over with the poster advertising the Nationals and said, "Russ, you're teaching this class—you ought to go down to this contest."

Five hundred people showed up to compete. After I qualified for the finals, Hobie said, "Look, if you ride for us, we'll give you a free T-shirt." It had always been one of my dreams to ride for Hobie. It was a prestigious thing. I ended up winning. I got the free T-shirt but never heard from Hobie again. I showed up late for work that day and lost my job and thought, *Well, you know what? This is the path I want to go down.*

Stacy Peralta was a member of the infamous Zephyr Boys, the world champion in '77, and *SkateBoarder*'s top male skater of 1979. He joined forces with George Powell to create Powell Peralta, one of the industry's premier brands, and scouted and mentored the most dominant skate team in history. He also essentially invented skateboard videos.

In the early 1990s, Stacy burned out and fled from skateboarding. He returned in 2001 with *Dogtown and Z-Boys*, a feature-length documentary that did the unprecedented by sparking skaters' interest in their own history. The film also reignited the shredding spark in Stacy, who can be spotted riding the Santa Monica skatepark where he and the Z-Boys started hopping fences to ride empty pools over thirty years ago.

Stacy Peralta, three wheels out, Paramount, 1978. **Photo:** James Cassimus

SP: When I was four, in 1962, a kid across the street from my grandfather had the classic skateboard scooter: an apple crate with stick handlebars bolted to a two-by-four with metal roller-skate wheels. I'd ride that down the sidewalk.

I saw the Tony the Tiger TV commercial that featured the Makaha team when I was around seven years old, and it knocked me out. I was aware, even as a kid, how incredibly unusual it was to see something like that on a cereal commercial. We were used to seeing the typical football hero eating a bowl of Wheaties. Here were kids doing head-stands, jumping over poles, skating in unison, doing wheelies.

When I was eight years old, I rode a borrowed red fiberglass Hobie skate-board, and the feeling of going up and down and turning really clicked. I remember thinking, *I love how this feels*. It felt very liberating.

At that point, skateboarding culture was 100 percent linked to surfing. Skateboarding did not exist—surfing did, and that was what we did. It was our way to surf all day and into the night. I got on Zephyr [*the local surf shop*] when I was fourteen as a surfer for the junior surf team. One day at a team meeting, Tony [*Alva*] said, "We have all these great skaters—why don't we start a skate team?" We got a T-shirt and a skateboard, and they started making fiberglass Zephyr boards. The senior Zephyr surf team was eighteen to twenty, and not one guy on it skate-boarded. It would have been weird if someone that old did.

When pool riding exploded in '75 and '76, the technology of skateboards exploded too, with wider trucks and urethane wheels, and skating developed its own culture outside the shadow of surfing, at least for me. All these dif-ferent factions were suddenly trying to define what skateboarding would become. Was it going to be freestyle? Was it going to be slalom? Was it going to be bank riding? *Nobody* thought it was going to be pool riding, which is the weirdest thing. And nobody imagined this thing called street skating.

Originally I loved all types of skat-ing, and we were encouraged to com-pete in all the events back then. It was *really* important to be a good all-around skater. It wasn't until the events became really specialized that I stopped slaloming and freestyling and it became all about pool riding for me, period. There just wasn't anything else any more. At that point, I could say, "I'm a skateboarder." I couldn't really say that when I was a kid. Then I was a surfer—I just happened to skateboard and love it. But you didn't say you were a skateboarder back then, you said you skateboarded.

But when I said I was a skate-boarder, people probably thought I was an idiot. They'd look at me with a blank stare. I didn't tell girls I did it. Skate-boarding always had the "Why would you waste your time doing that?" stigma. If Austin [*Stacy's sixteen-year-old son*] spent the greater part of his day riding a pogo stick, I'd think there was some-thing wrong with him. That's the image skateboarding had—it was as trivial as a pogo stick. I can't believe my parents let me—they must have thought, *Why would anybody spend four hours doing this? What benefit are you going to get from this?*

The absence of adult supervision made you feel that much more marginalized. When you went into the other [*nonskating*] world, you didn't talk about it, couldn't share it. Skateboarding was a closed little world. At that time, if you surfed you were outside [*the school peer group*] anyway. It was completely antisocial. But skateboarding was even further on the margin.

IN THE DOGTOWN ARTICLES FOR *SKATEBOARDER* I WAS IN, THE KIDS WERE A BUNCH OF RATS. YOUR PARENTS AREN'T GOING TO LOOK AT THAT AND THINK THEIR KID IS GOING TO RUN EXXON SOME DAY.

There was a certain low self-esteem that we all…well, I know *I* suffered from because I chose this activity that didn't get parental support. It didn't even get parental *interest*. Deep down, I questioned why I did this. *I guess I'm kind of a loser*, I thought. *But I love it enough that I'll never stop.*

Being a skateboarder was one of the things that put me in touch with who I was. When I skateboarded, I felt, *Yes, this is who I am*. It made me feel good about myself that I could do it well. Style was the most important thing, because skateboarding wasn't technical back then, so the only thing you had going for you was style. You practiced maneuvers over and over and over again, because you wanted to get them connected to who you were. When you did a great Bertlemann turn, man… it was a gesture of who you were. Once you've experienced style, it's always a part of you and carries over, influencing everything in your life.

I was sixteen when I started getting in the magazines, and it was absolute heaven and nirvana. From that point forward, I wanted to be in every issue, and if I wasn't, I was angry. It made me feel great. I loved it. Every guy in there loved it. My parents never said this, but I'm assuming they looked at it the same way I would if Austin got in a pogo-stick magazine: *How long is this going to last? OK, it's kind of cool, but it's trivial.* In the Dogtown articles for *SkateBoarder* I was in, the kids were a bunch of rats. Your parents aren't going to look at that and think their kid is going to run Exxon some day. I don't know if it really pleased them, other than temporary fascination: *This is a curious thing, but will it lead to anything?*

No.

Dave Hackett was just a little stoner surf-rat skater when he started bombing his neighborhood hills in Malibu, California. He channeled the anger and emotion that swelled from his troubled childhood (his brother eventually killed his mother) into his skating. Unlike Tony Hawk and Rodney Mullen, Hackett remained in the skate scene for decades as an icon of style rather than an innovator of progressive tricks. He won pool contests in the late '70s, and in the '80s he personified the surf-skate style.

Today, Hackett throws out his age in conversation, almost as a taunt. He's closing in on fifty, but he still buzzed the skate world when he showed up at Tony Hawk's loop; "manned up," as he put it; and rolled around the structure that has broken the best in the business. Then he returned and, in typical Hackett style, looped shirt-less, padless, helmetless—and in jeans.

Dave Hackett, slash grind, Gonzales pool, 1986. **Photo:** James Castaneda

DH: Back in 1963, skating was a big fad, and by 1965 my parents had bought my sister, my brother, and me red Roller Derby skateboards. We made an obstacle course in our garage—tunnels with blankets, things like that—and we'd kneeboard around. My brother and I eventually took it outside to the sidewalk.

I was only six years old, and I didn't get serious about skateboarding until I was nine, when I learned how to surf. My skateboard transported me to the beach. I lived above Topanga Canyon, in Malibu. I'd ditch school at nine and ten years old and skate down to Topanga.

Every day we would meet up at the top of the mesa and get completely stoned out of our minds. I started doing the hills on clay wheels when I was eleven. I started getting stoned when I was thirteen. We had about fifteen streets, all on a 7 percent grade, leading down to the street that dumped out on Pacific Coast Highway. All the guys who lived up there—about twenty or thirty of us—skateboarded those hills every day.

The clay wheels would break apart, and I'd go through a set of wheels in a couple of weeks. The wheels just exploded when they wore out, and all the loose bearings would spill out. It was a bummer. But you could buy clay wheels on Sure-Grip trucks on a Hobie super-surfer board down at Malibu Toys 'n' Sports for five dollars.

Cadillac and Rollersport were the first urethane wheels, and they came out in '74. When I got my first set of them, I was fourteen and getting lit, just stoned out of my mind, and skateboarding those hills twenty, thirty times a day.

My friend had a Baja Bug, and he thought it'd be funny to see how fast I could go on my board with Rollersport wheels. At around 35 miles per hour, I got massive speed wobbles and I had to dive away from the car so I wouldn't get run over by the slicks on the back. I ate holy shit. My dad took that skateboard and sawed it in half in the garage.

My parents bought my brother and me Bahne skateboards with Cadillac wheels for forty dollars. I immediately took mine to Paul Revere Junior High School in Santa Monica. I was the only kid with Cadillac wheels, and everybody was like, "Wow!" They had heard of them and seen them in the magazines, but nobody had one. This one kid came up to me, an older guy, and said, "You have the new Bahne with the Cadillac wheels! Dude! That's awesome! Can I try it?"

"Yeah, try it out."

He grabs it—*bam!*—he's gone. Gone. I stood there for a second thinking, *Is he coming back?* Then I started to cry.

Everybody there laughed at me.

When I came home without that board…I got a beating. I was grounded. They told me I was done with skateboarding and I was never to go back to Revere. It took a while, but I convinced my parents to buy me another Bahne, and of course I went back to Revere. This time I hitchhiked there with my best friend, Chad McQueen. I went down the big hill, and my back Chicago truck broke. I fell, broke my arm. Chad panicked and called an ambulance. My parents met me at the Santa Monica Emergency Hospital: "You are so fucking done with skateboarding."

Steve Olson straight-up freaked out the skateboard industry. A vert hero born from the Henry Hester Pro Bowl Series, he was an unpredicted icon for magazine and skate-company men used to controlling the direction of skateboarding. The emergence of the "pro pool rider" finalized the legitimacy of vertical terrain, and when the readers of *SkateBoarder* voted Olson the top male skater of 1978, he triggered a quake that shook the main-stays' slalom and freestyle china off the wall.

But skate icons are as much personality as talent. Olson's embrace of punk, a movement that, like skating, celebrated disorder and the underdog, severed the indus-try's ties to the mellow '70s surfer mentality.

Olson flared up and flamed out, a victim of bad timing, as skating died quickly after a burst of popularity. But his style is still stamped on skateboarding. Today, many skaters look as if they attended the Olson School of Style, while he looks, acts, and skates as authentically punk as ever.

Steve Olson, rock 'n' roll, Big O, 1979. Photo: James Cassimus

SO: Skateboards were like a toy. I was six in '67, living in the East Bay, and for Christmas my brother and I got steel-wheeled Roller Derbies. We'd ride on our knees, our ass, our belly—it was just transportation. We'd shoot the hills of the East Bay and just get slammed.

I moved down to Long Beach in the fourth grade, in the early '70s, and if you weren't surfing, you were skating. I started making my own shit a few years later in wood shop. Your skateboard had something to do with who you were, and you glued surf pictures on it or whatever.

The mid-'70s were dramatic. Skateboarding was still toy-based, but it was totally about customizing and putting on round polka dots and gluing sandpaper discs or whatever you wanted. It was dope. It was so ill back then. You were always trying to make something dope. I still make my own skateboards.

Around '76 and '77, skateboard parks started popping up by my house in Orange County. We had Skateopia, Concrete Wave, Paramount, and Big O. My brother, who was four years older, worked at Concrete Wave, and then it was just done—that was where I broke out. I'd go to work with my brother and skate.

I was skating more than surfing at that point, for sure. It just happened—there was not a choice. The surf wasn't always good, but the skateparks were popping up and they were always new and sick. Then they put in a pool at Concrete Wave, and it was fucking on. That's when I really learned how to fucking destroy shit.

George [*Powell*] came to the skatepark with a briefcase with two sets of wheels and asked this one Japanese cat, a photographer, who were the really good guys. The photographer said Ray Bones and me, and we rode his wheels, and they were pretty sick. He's always made amazing wheels.

Then the Santa Cruz team came down to Concrete Wave for a contest, and we smoked them. I skated freestyle, slalom—everything. You had to be able to win the overall point total if you were anything.

I got on the Santa Cruz team, and things totally changed. They had a team manager, there were jerseys—it was totally legit. We had a motor home and shit. It was sweet: free stuff, traveling places, and getting pictures in the mags—it was dope. I didn't care about the jerseys. I wasn't really fashion-forward at all.

I went to Spring Valley [*the first pool contest*] and represented Santa Cruz, and I was from Southern California. There was always the NorCal against SoCal thing, and it was a joke. I did good for them so they were stoked, and I was definitely going to get a pro model.

People at school didn't know I was a champion skater. I dropped out before that could happen. I didn't go back for my twelfth year. I got my diploma from adult ed. I went to other contests [*he won the first overall Henry Hester Pro Bowl Series at age sixteen*]. I was getting money from contest winnings and matching. I lived at home. I didn't have rent or any of that bullshit. I was making 800 bucks a month salary from Santa Cruz. I bought some stupid Porsche thing. Skating was cool.

Steve Alba has been running away from angry homeowners for more than a quarter-century. He's a special-forces commander, using everything from airplanes to earthquake-disaster maps to locate empty backyard pools. For Steve, the hunt flavors his skating, but he's also unfortunately a primo personification of skateboarding's limp sense of history.

Salba isn't a random elder champ—he won the first-ever pro pool contest—who returned to rolling because skateboarding has blown up. This is a skateboarder who never stopped shredding, even though consistent coverage and major sponsorships dried up years ago. A middle-age man who still lives in the Inland Empire in California and spends weeks reconning a pool, draining it, and tearing it up with his friends, he loves skating more than most.

SA: In '74, when I started skating, we just rode whatever boards we could get—shitty, loose-ball-bearing nightmares. Then urethane wheels arrived, and I had a Grentec plastic board, a Hobie Header board. Within six months, we went from piece-of-crap boards to precision bearings, and *SkateBoarder* came out. It seemed like everything was possible.

I skated my first pool on a skateboard when I was in seventh grade, in '75. It was the Central Pool down on Stoner Alley. A couple of Mexican guys lived at the end of this alley and had their little gang, and on the other end of the alley were the hippie–white pride guys. The lower half belonged to the Mexicans and the top, the hippie dudes. Sometimes you'd see brawling.

One day I saw my buddy's older brother and his friends flip their boards into their hands and run down the alley. At the fourth house, they jumped the fence. It was an abandoned house. We watched them leave and went to see what they'd been doing. We had no idea how to skate in a pool. We slammed all the time, flipping out, hitting our heads, elbows. We didn't know how to kickturn, so for the first three months we just carved the scum line.

After four or five sessions at the pool, the big brother caught us: "What are you guys doing here?" He didn't really dig what we were doing at first, but after a while he got into it. He and his friends could carve over the light. I don't know if he knew anything more about skating, but he had *Creem* magazine and turned us on to Kiss and Bowie and Alice Cooper. As far I was concerned, he was the hippest guy in the world.

Halfway-decent boards were coming out by the summer of '75. That year was really pivotal for me. I was still playing sports and really into baseball and football. My teammates were like, "What are you doing?" In '77 skateboarding hit really hard—everybody had a skateboard—but before that, in '75, people tripped out on me doing something different. And skating is way different than playing baseball.

A girl I knew from school said, "This house next to me has a pool. and the people just moved out." It was on Bel Air Street, so we called it the Bel Air pool. That summer, because of the drought, people couldn't fill up their pools if they were emptied. Pretty soon, we had five pools to skate.

Once we got into pools, that was all we wanted to ride. We'd take the Omni-Trans, a local bus that only cost a quarter to go across town. When we went to the L pool, we tripped out, because there was already a full-on scene. There were twenty people, easy, skating. It was full of all these dudes we never knew skated. I was around thirteen, and these guys skating were sixteen, seventeen, eighteen. Our group of friends was kind of okay skaters by then. But the older guys still picked on us. It was tough love, and that made you get really good fast. If you could keep up with the big guys, then you were some hot shit.

There are many legends in skateboarding, gifted freaks who have taken the level of skating to a higher plane. **<u>Lance</u> <u>Mountain</u>** will straight-up inform you that he's not one of them. Although talented, he earned his legend status by personifying the fun of skating better than anybody.

A member of the Bones Brigade, the most popular and dominant team in skateboarding history, he attracted a massive following because of what he represented—the normal dude who skates purely for fun. As famous for his hilarious slams and contest dorking as he was for his contest victories, Lance deflated the hot air from an industry that can at times take itself too seriously. Most tricks date, but the reason we all started skating doesn't, and that's a main reason why many of the Powell Peralta videos featuring Lance continue to sell, decades past the standard shelf life.

Lance Mountain, frontside invert, Upland, 1983. Photo: Grant Brittain

LM: In 1974, when I was ten, my friend Enrique gave me his old board with clay wheels, and it was garbage. We played tag on it, sat in boxes on top of the board and went down the hill until we hit this patch of ivy and flew out. We even pushed to school, which was five miles away. I've had a board ever since.

I didn't do *any* other activities. I tried out for football, and I was terrible. I didn't like organized sports, because they told you what to do and if you messed up, you were letting somebody down. And they were hard. If you couldn't hit a baseball, you were bad. At that time, if you skateboarded, you were auto- matically good, because most people couldn't even stand on one. But I didn't think about what it meant to me. I got on it, and it gave me fun.

I WAS SO OBSESSED THAT TEACHERS WERE CONCERNED, AND THEY SHOULD HAVE BEEN – I DON'T HAVE A LOT OF SKILLS THAT YOU SHOULD HAVE.

Around '78 I was around thirteen, so it was cool to skateboard, because it was what little kids did. I don't remember a time after stepping on my skateboard that I wasn't doing it or thinking about it all the time. Any time I did a poetry assignment for school, it was about skateboarding. I once tried to pass off a drawing of Stacy Peralta doing a kickturn as a history paper. I was so obsessed that teachers were concerned, and they should have been—I don't have a lot of skills that you should have. I have horrible people skills. I never look anybody in the eye. I'm not very open. I think I got that from skating, because I always felt like I was useless.

Teachers would say, "Aren't you too old to play on that toy?" My parents were like that too until they saw me enter a contest and I won or whatever. But they were still worried about how I'd make a living.

In '80, George Orton asked me to ride for Variflex. I said no: "If I ever rode for anybody, I'd want to ride for Powell."

But Stevie [*Caballero*] had already come down to our local skatepark, and he was like, "This kid bugs. He's just following us around the skatepark trying to be better than us." I was just excited and thought if they saw me skate, they might put me on the team. And really, guys like Stevie were just getting to be known at that time. They weren't [*Tony*] Alva, they were just the new kids and I wanted to be a part of that.

But Variflex said they were going on a national tour and wanted to take me. Amateurs never went on tours back then, so I rode for them. When we got home, it just seemed like everyone who skated was gone. In one summer, skating changed. The Variflex team was done—all the pros had quit. And then Variflex called me and asked if I wanted to go pro.

I was in high school and had a job as a night watchman so I could skate. I was watching an apartment complex to make sure nobody stole wood, which is the funnest job for a skateboarder who's building a ramp in his backyard. But I didn't steal any wood. I sat in my car and drew ideas for my graphics for Variflex.

It was definitely a dream of mine to turn pro, but by now it was a dead dream. It wasn't as if I had come rushing into anything—nothing was left. The next generation of skaters was all that was left. It was more like the companies just said, "Oh, I guess you guys get to be pro now." There wasn't any contract, and I think they paid me fifty cents a board.

So I had my pro board from Variflex, and I eventually got a job at Variflex screening boards, though I never screened my own, only junky ones that it wouldn't matter if I messed up. I remember thinking, *So this is what being pro is*. I didn't care. I got a royalty check for fourteen bucks.

In 1983, when I was around seventeen, Variflex said they were going to discontinue pro models and just be a toy company. I was bummed. I was getting out of high school and had to make money. I was friends with Stevie by now, and he and Stacy came to pick me up for a contest at Palmdale. I had been telling my mom how Stacy was a pro skater with a great company. So Stacy shows up and she asked, "Do you have any ideas for my son? He respects what you've done, and he always wants to be involved with skateboarding."

Stacy offered me a job at Powell for $200 a month. I'd get on the team and maybe work into his job, but I wouldn't have a pro model. Better to be on Powell without a board than what I had. After the release of *Bones Brigade Video*

Show in 1984, skaters began to ask for my pro model. Stacy said, "Everybody is asking for your pro model—what do you think about having one again?"

I REPRESENTED THAT SKATEBOARDING WAS FUN TO DO BY BEING TERRIBLE AT IT.

I had accepted that I wasn't going to have one anymore. I *always* knew, when I got on Powell, exactly what I represented. I was the [*normal*] guy getting on this [*elite*] team. I knew that most skaters weren't as talented as the Powell team—most of them were like me. I was a real skateboarder, not a gifted skateboarder. I represented that skateboarding was fun to do by being terrible at it.

That was the point of skateboarding: to stay young and have fun. It was never, in my mind, this thing to do to get in the Olympics or be famous or win first place. It was what you did to excite yourself and have friends and screw around and be immature, and progressing and winning allowed you to stay a part of it. Skateboarding totally stunts you. It keeps you immature. There was a fear of growing up. Still is.

Kevin Harris might as well have skated on the moon for all the skate coverage his home country of Canada received in the late 1970s. Paying his own way to contests in California, he eventually earned a slot on Powell Peralta's Bones Brigade and was ranked second in the world for freestyle. "Kevin Harris is one of the greatest skateboarders in the world—period," Stacy Peralta says. "When Kevin rides his board, he becomes one with it."

While still a top pro in the mid-'80s, Kevin started Ultimate Skateboard Distribution, and from that success created the Richmond Skate Ranch, the first indoor skate-park with a connected mini ramp. It was the location of the first pro mini ramp contest and became an international destination. Kevin lost over 50 Gs with RSR but felt he should give back to the skate community that had given him so much. He recently paid a contractor $40,000 to pour a polished-cement skateboard area in his back-yard near Vancouver, where he skates daily.

Kevin Harris, one-wheel manual, 1987. **Photo:** Grant Brittain

KH: It was '75, and I was thirteen, living in Richmond, British Columbia. One day a friend, Don, showed up at my house with a skateboard he had brought back from a California vacation. He did a few simple tricks, and instantly I wanted one of my own. My dad drove me down to Collegiate Sports, and we bought a skateboard for twenty bucks.

My friends on my street all bought boards, and we skated every day. Don came back a few days later, and I was skating regular-footed, which felt natural, but Don said, "You're totally skating the wrong way. Everybody in California skates with their right foot forward." Don had been to California, so he was the expert. I switched my stance.

In the spring of '76, the G&S team was skating at Dairy Queens across Canada to promote skateboarding. The big star at my local demo was Doug "Pineapple" Saladino, who was close to my age. They wore uniforms of yellow shirts, red shorts, Vans, red kneepads, long hair—there was no mistaking that they were from California. Of course, it was raining during the demo. It rains all the time in Richmond, and I couldn't understand what the big deal was. The announcer would say, "This will be harder in the rain, but let's see if Pineapple can make his Pineapple Flip!"

I started living on my skateboard. I dropped baseball, riding motorbikes—everything was chucked out. My baseball coach even called my parents to try and convince me to keep playing. If it was sunny, I skated outside; if it rained, I'd skate in my open carport; if the rain blew in, I'd skate inside on the thick shag carpet. I learned single kickflips, double kickflips, M-80s, all on carpet.

In the summer of '76, I saw my first contest, in Vancouver. It was just Canadian skaters, and it included all these crazy events, like high-jump, cross-country, barrel jumping, slalom, freestyle. The skaters on my street got together and made a crappy backwoods version of the contest. We made a high-jump bar out of a hockey stick and two trash cans. We stole warning pylons and used them as slalom cones.

I dreamed of getting sponsored, but at the time, I always felt like a second-class citizen, being a Canadian skateboarder. There was no such thing as a real professional skateboarder from Canada. Over the years, I won the Canadian freestyle championship five times, but you knew Canada was like a miniature skate-world version of California.

By 1980, everybody I knew had stopped skating. I'd skate by myself, or with one friend who liked ramps. I continued traveling to California for contests, because that was the only way left to interact with skaters. In 1982, when I was nineteen, I entered a pro contest by a fluke, because there weren't enough skaters to hold pro contests separate from the amateurs. Stacy Peralta introduced himself. "We're going out for dinner—do you want to come with us?" he asked.

Of course, I said yes. I loved Powell Peralta, and who wouldn't want to eat with other skateboarders in the early '80s? "I really liked your skating," Stacy said, "and we'd love for you to ride for Powell."

That changed everything. Even though it meant nothing to almost everybody in my life, it verified that I'd been on the right track all this time.

There was no such thing as "streetstyle" when **Tommy Guerrero** skated his hometown San Francisco hills, blending the bombing with freestyle and faux-vert maneuvers and creating his own Frankenstein monster at the same time as pioneers like Mark Gonzales and Natas Kaupas were developing theirs.

Tommy ground his name in skate history with his smooth style and his victory at the first pro street contest as an unknown in 1983. Powell Peralta released *Future Primitive* in 1985, and Tommy's part was the first recognized street skating section in a video. As skaters everywhere hit rewind, Tommy's few minutes of shredding San Francisco proved more powerful than any first-place trophy.

Tommy continues to work with his old friends Jim Thiebaud and Mark Gonzales at various skateboard companies under the Deluxe label.

Tommy Guerrero, one-footed Japan, Oceanside, 1986. **Photo:** Grant Brittain

TG: I lived on a hill on 17th Avenue, and in '75, I was about nine. My friend had a little Black Knight, one of the first clay-wheel skateboards, with a little knight graphic. It was very cool, but he wasn't that into it, so he gave me the board. From then on I was totally sprung. My older brother got into skating at the same time, and my mom nurtured it any way she could.

Urethane was already happening, but we weren't privy to it. A friend of ours made a skateboard out of an old Formica table and roller-skate wheels. We were still like Neanderthals, not even upright yet.

I never got into any sports, ever. Nothing. I was never into any of that shit. It seemed that all my life, because I was really small, I got a bunch of grief. I was always a good six inches shorter than everybody, if not more. When I started skating, of course, I got shit for that. When I got into the punk scene, of course, I got shit again.

Skating was every single day—all day long. We built backyard ramps out of four-by-eight plywood sheets, and I was out there at night trying to learn little backside airs with a glove on, because my hand would get so raw from doing it for eight hours.

SkateBoarder was the bible, right? We went over that with a fine-tooth comb. It was impossible to figure out what the riders in the pictures were doing. There's photos of Jay Adams looking like he's doing some sort of an Andrecht edger thing. What the fuck is that? A bail shot would kind of look like a frontside ollie in a pool or something.

In '76 we had gotten decent skateboards, and Alameda, the first skatepark in the Bay Area, opened. It was insane: "Holy crap! We see these in the magazines and here it is!"

Other NorCal parks opened up: Winchester, Milpitas, Campbell. When skateboarding was going under and the skateparks closed in the early '80s, we'd just go outside and skate. Just because the parks closed, it wasn't like you said, "Oh, I'll go and play football."

YOU KNOW HOW PROGRESSION IS – IT HAPPENS REALLY NATURALLY. IT'S NOT LIKE YOU SUDDENLY ANNOUNCE, "I'M GOING TO PIONEER THE OLLIE"...

We'd mimic grinding coping by grinding curbs. That's how Hazzards and all those goofy tricks came around, right? Street skaters wanted to become vert skaters, but they couldn't hang, couldn't hack it. You just adapted the stuff you learned at the skateparks to street.

You know how progression is—it happens really naturally. It's not like you suddenly announce, "I'm going to pioneer the ollie" or some shit. Most of it is accidental. Tricks evolve from bailing, or getting sketchy and barely pulling something and then trying to re-create it. Back then, it was so much more diverse—running and jumping off a car was considered a trick. That wasn't my thing. I was mixing the freestyle with the street shit, doing fingerflips and that stuff off ramps.

Rodney [Mullen] started doing the high stationary ollie, and we gradually learned it. The ollie revolutionized hill skating—you're flying down a hill, up a curb, pop, over a bush, whatever. That opened the doors, opened up everything. Your perspective completely changed: "Hmm, wait a minute, that is not an obstacle anymore, in the sense of being in your way. It's actually an object that can be used." It changed skating for the better to this day, obviously.

Skating became utilitarian. Skate from A to B, or to the punk show or whatever. It became more of the DIY thing. We built a quarterpipe and used to drag it up the block from my house to a schoolyard.

To some degree, skateboarding had lost a little direction and I was a little disillusioned. I always skated, but there was no skate mag, no skateparks. The *Thrasher* streetstyle contest put skateboarding back in focus, in the sense that there was a whole movement. [*Tommy won that first professional street competition.*] I was only hanging out with a few people who skated at that time. At that contest, it was like, *Cool, there's a bunch of people still skating and totally into it.*

Street skating wasn't a term yet. It was coined for the *Thrasher* contest, probably as a marketing tool. It was just, "Let's go skate, Miley…." It wasn't "Let's go street skate!" "Let's go ditch skate!" "Let's go slalom skate!"

I got on Madrid after the contest, through Tom Groholski and Chuck Treece.

The Madrid people were like, "What does he do?" Street skating wasn't recognized. They told me that they wanted me to return the boards they gave me, under the guise of seeing how they were wearing out. I think they just wanted to make sure I wasn't selling their stuff.

The day before the second street contest at Golden Gate Park, in '84, all the pros in town for the contest were skating Joe Lopes's ramp. I slammed really hard and was done. Me and my friends went and got a twelve-pack, sat on the roof, and watched. Stacy [Peralta] came up and said, "I like the way you skate."

I was looking around, like, *Who are you talking to?* I had met Stacy during a Fort Mason contest around '76 or '77. I had seen the quintessential Stacy photo in *SkateBoarder* of him doing 360s with his hair flying out. I saw him at the contest doing 360s and I was like, *"It's that guy!"* I met him because I used to be able to do a bunch of 360s for a little monkey and he said, "Hey, man, that's rad!" He'll never remember it, but I always remember it. So this was the second meeting, and I was like, *"Wait a sec. Whoa. You're talking to me?"* He was one of my heroes, so coming from him, I was tripping out.

The next day, at the contest, my brother told me that Stacy had talked to him about me riding for Powell Peralta. We had always called Powell "the Dream Team." I thought my brother was kidding.

Fact: Skateboarding would look entirely different today if Florida native **Rodney Mullen** had picked up golf clubs like his father wanted him to. In more than a decade of freestyle contests, he lost only once—and the consensus is that he was merely being judged against himself, because he fell in his final run, something he rarely did. He created the flatland ollie and the kickflip, two tricks that broke the access code, allowing the urban environment to be used by modern street skaters.

Then pro freestyle withered in the early 1990s, died, and blew away, and Rodney was the sole survivor of an ancient race. He not only picked up street skating—reluctantly, at first—but won, at age thirty-six, the 2002 Transworld Reader's Poll Award for favorite skater. Rodney and Tony Hawk belong to that exclusive club of skaters over forty who still create and land maneuvers that kids stumble over.

RM: My older sister was a surfer, and her friends hung out at our house and skated. It was 1976, and I was the goofy little kid who wanted to hang out with them. They were disarming, more of the reject guys in a sense, a little bit on the fringe—definitely not people my folks were stoked to see her hanging around with.

I was ten years old and liked that they were all different types. It was really easy to characterize, for example, the guys who played baseball or the people in school cliques, and I never really felt like I belonged to them. I loved how everything was loose—no confining, no regimentation. It was so accepting. There wasn't some guy with a whistle and a stopwatch giving the sense of being measured.

My dad wasn't stoked on it. He said he didn't want me to skate because I might get hurt, but it was definitely the culture—he called my sister's friends a bunch of bums who weren't going anywhere in life. I wasn't allowed to have a skateboard, and I had never wanted to participate in anything more. My friend gave me a *SkateBoarder* magazine, and it felt like smuggling. I stared at the pages, and the need for a skateboard incubated in me.

My dad finally agreed to let me skateboard on New Year's Eve 1976, but with stipulations. There were always stipulations. I'm not sure why I hold on to skateboarding so hard, but the stipulations probably had a lot to do with it. Until I moved out of my parents' house, I skateboarded under the threat that it could always be taken away— and that made my skating time precious.

I MADE PADS FOR UNDER THE WHEELS AND PUT ITS NAME AND BIRTHDAY ON A CARD UNDER IT.

I try to not use the possessive and say "my" a lot, but it was *my* skateboard. I made a place for it at night, and while I wouldn't call it a bed, it was close. I made pads for under the wheels and put its name and birthday on a card under it. I set it there every night. That skateboard was the biggest sense of "mine" that I'd ever experienced.

Skateboarding gave me a purpose, and in every spare moment, I skated. I hung out with other skaters at the beginning, but once I got my own board I kind of stopped. I had my own board and didn't need them anymore to get the feeling out of it. I just wanted to skate. Skating was *very* personal for me. Even today, no one is allowed to watch me skate. Period. I *love* the time when no one can watch. I'm a night creature. [*Rodney often skates from midnight until 6:30 in the morning.*]

It sounds fruity, but my memories started having footprints, tangibility, when I started skateboarding. I look back and don't really have any indelible memories before that. Things weren't always good around the house, and I'd deal with those problems by just skating. It completely enveloped me, and everything would dissipate. It was like diving into water—all sound would disappear, and I'd just hear my own heartbeat.

This immersion became an issue with my father. I was eleven years old and had been skating for about a year, and I'd feel guilty if I didn't skate enough. He said, "Look, this is stunting your growth as a person. You don't communicate with anyone, and I'm afraid you're going to have a lot of problems later on in life." But he let me keep skating. The local shop sponsored me pretty quickly, and they tricked me into entering my first contest. They said they wouldn't drive me home unless I skated. They literally pushed me out into the contest area, and I won.

I got on Walker skateboards when I was still eleven, and on Powell Peralta the next year. I started skating at Sensation Basin, my local park. It was fun skating the big bowl or the little half-pipe with other people, but I'd freestyle alone, because hardly anyone else did.

Skateboarding became this Linus blanket for me after I won the Oceanside [amateur nationals] contest when I was twelve. My dad began weighing down on me and wanted me to quit skating and start playing golf, "a sport where athletes really compete." Things grew darker, and skating was my only thing, so I held it that much tighter. I was skating five hours a day—very strictly defined. If I went to the bathroom, I stopped the timer on my Casio.

In 1980, Stacy [Peralta] invited me to enter my first pro contest, but Powell Peralta couldn't afford a ticket to Oasis skatepark in San Diego. My dad bought my plane ticket, because he said he wanted me to have my last fling.

Winning was not on my mind. At the contest, I was just tripping out on seeing all my heroes in one spot. I skated

very differently than they did, and in the end I felt weird about beating all those guys. Being put "above" them didn't feel right, and it changed my whole spectrum. It felt *really* wrong.

I woke up the next morning knowing very clearly that skating was over for me. I had never officially been told I was on Powell, and I asked Stacy if I was on the team. He laughed: "Of course you're on!" He gave me the special Bones Brigade patch. It was a neat closure.

That weekend became part of my core, and even at that age I realized that it would shape me for a long, long time. I saved everything from the trip: wrappers, airline-ticket stubs, receipts. My dad's reaction to my win was: "That's fine." It was like being the best yo-yo guy in the neighborhood: Who cares? "I've always told you that you were a great athlete," he said. "Now let's do it where real people compete, not against a bunch of bums. It's not something to be really proud of, Rodney. I'm glad you had a good experience and met your heroes, but it's time to move on." It was sort of like being the tallest man among jockeys.

I organized all my skate stuff for hours, put it all in a trash bag, and hid it in the depths of my closet. It's where I would have kept my porn if I'd had any. Then everything just felt numb.

I tried to focus on what would be the next aspect of my life, but I had no goal except homework, so my homework was sparkling. I had nothing to tether me to what I was—skateboarding was it. When I lost that, I lost my sense of self. It wasn't like happy or sad—there was nothing, and this lethargy overwhelmed me. What was the point of getting up?

Three days later, a skate magazine called our house for an interview. It wasn't even a magazine, it was at best a 'zine. But my father heard me give this interview and said, "I can't believe this—they're calling you from across the country and they're going to print an interview with you all over the world." I think he realized that making me quit skating was taking a greater toll than he had imagined it would. He said I could skate again.

I THINK HE REAL-IZED THAT MAKING ME QUIT SKATING WAS TAKING A GREATER TOLL THAN HE HAD IMAGINED IT WOULD.

Within minutes, I was outside skating. I had always known that skating was for the moment. It was never going to become a career or a job—there was no money or contracts or promises. Powell couldn't even afford a flight out to a contest. Skating was always going to be short-lived, ephemeral, and you had to make the most of it while you could. My future was kind of laid out: I was going to college and then I'd become a doctor or an engineer or something like that. High school, at best, would be the end of skateboarding, and by college, of course, it'd be over.

For a newer skater to understand **Tony Hawk**, the post-900, post-Playstation pixilated presence must be peeled away. But that's a difficult feat, considering Tony was the one who popped the current mainstream's skate cherry by landing the first ever 900 on national TV in '99. That and his easily understood contest domination made him the unofficial face of skateboarding for the outside world.

Nearing the quarter-century mark as a pro, a competition-retired Tony continues to innovate and make other skaters thank the Skate God they don't have to worry about his contest runs anymore. But the drive is still there, redlining. Recently, while skating his backyard cement skatepark near San Diego with a friend, the friend piled hard. "I know it hurts to slam," Tony said as his buddy limped toward him, "but doesn't it feel good in a way? You know you're still pushing yourself and learning."

Tony Hawk, 540 over gap, desert, 2001. Photo: Grant Brittain

TH: Around 1980, Denise Barter, the manager for Dogtown Skateboards, came to my home skatepark, Oasis, for a contest. This wasn't the original Dogtown, with Tony Alva and Stacy [Peralta] and Jay Adams—this was the second incarnation.

I knew who Jay and Stacy were, but as far as I was concerned, the dudes that were skating pools were Steve Olsen, Duane Peters, and Eddie Elguera. It was a generational shift into an era that was unknown, because skating had just died and skateparks were going under, but there was a new breed.

My dad was talking to Denise and realized that they didn't have a place to stay, so they stayed with us. It was Mike Smith, Denise, and her dog. While they were at our place, I bugged them about how to get sponsored. "Well, you've got to learn a few more tricks," they said. "You should learn to do inverts."

Of course, I spent all my time trying to learn inverts, and the next time they came to town, I said, "Look! I can do inverts!" You could just barely call them inverts.

There was no protocol to getting sponsored. It was just, "OK, we'll give you some stuff." Being sponsored meant that I got some random equipment every once in a while. My first sponsored equipment was Mike Smith's used skateboard. Supposedly I was sponsored by Indy, but all I ever got was one hanger. I was doing well in my age division, and I asked the Tracker team manager if I could get some trucks. I wasn't asking to get sponsored—I just needed trucks, because mine were trashed, and it was such a small community that you knew everybody

at contests. But they did end up sponsoring me.

Now that I was sponsored, I entered the Gold Cup contests, and through my naive twelve-year-old eyes, they were heavy events. Every contest I had entered before that had been divided into age divisions or your skill level—this was just straight "amateurs."

After a few months, the calls from Dogtown were getting fewer and farther between. They eventually said, "The wood manufacturer is down in San Diego. You can just go down there and get blank boards from them." What I didn't realize then was that Dogtown wasn't selling any boards, so they were hardly screening any.

One night the phone rang, and it was Stacy. Powell Peralta had the most respected team at the time, for sure. He'd only talked to me one other time, at a contest, when he asked how Dogtown was treating me. I was shocked that he even knew who I was or who my sponsor was, so I just said, "Fine." I didn't even know how a sponsored skater was supposed to be treated.

He told me that Dogtown had gone out of business and wondered if I wanted to come up to L.A. and skate Marina skatepark. Stacy gave me an experimental Caballero model to try out. I skated the keyhole and jumped the channel backside, and Stacy did his laughing thing and said he couldn't believe I'd done that. I was doing it late-grab, which was a new thing at the time. After a while, he said, "We'd really like to sponsor you."

I got home, and my dad asked how it went. I said, "Good. I guess I'm riding for Powell." There was no formal deal.

Mike Valley was a wrecking ball that slammed into skateboarding. Discovered in a parking-lot street session in 1986 when he was fifteen, he eventually changed board design, the skater look, and how the industry operated. His opening shot in the Powell Peralta video *Public Domain*, in 1988, was alarming: pale shaved head, beaten military-surplus cargo pants, and mismatched shoes that looked as if they'd spent the night in a blender. A socially awkward punk urban guerrilla, Mike V. erased the traces of surf culture in skating and gave a face to the alienation skaters felt during the 1980s.

He left Powell, then the most popular skate brand, for World Industries, a start-up launched by Steve Rocco and Rodney Mullen with paper-bag cash from a loan shark.

A few years later, the industry dismissed Valley as washed up, and his stomach was filling with blood from an ulcer. He would return with a mission instead of a career. It was skating that had changed his life, not sponsorship and pro endorsements, and he wanted to pass on that message to the masses.

Mike Valley, wallride, School W., 1986. **Photo:** Grant Brittain

STALEFISH

MV: I had seen a few hippyish-looking dudes riding a hill by my house, but skateboarding didn't really show up on my radar until the sixth grade. I took a skateboarding book out of my school library, and this kid saw it and said he knew everything about skateboarding. He was a kid I'd never have normally talked to, but I went over to his house and looked at his skateboards. I tried to ride one on his street, but it was so rough that vibrations went through my feet and legs. It sucked. Wasn't fun at all.

We were invited to a sixth-grade Halloween party, and one of us got in a fight and we got kicked out. We'd ridden our skateboards to the party but forgot them at the top of the driveway.

Somebody screamed, "You forgot your skateboards, faggots!"

I started to turn around to go back and get it, but it was already airborne. The older cousin of the kid having the party threw it from the top of the drive-way, and it crossed the whole yard. As I started to turn around, my board came out of the air and hit me in the neck so hard that I hit the ground and couldn't get up. My neck was so fucked up. When I did get up, I eventually staggered home and didn't want to have anything to do with skateboarding.

It wasn't until my freshman year in 1984 that I got interested again. I was walking down the street and saw this kid I knew carrying a skateboard. He was carrying a Sims Hosoi Rising Sun. Something was coming off the board and speaking to me. The graphics and the look of the board gave off this vibe. I remember the whole scene in slow motion. It was kind of like an awakening.

HE WAS CARRYING A SIMS HOSOI RISING SUN. SOME-THING WAS COMING OFF THE BOARD AND SPEAKING TO ME.

I had gone into my freshman year without any friends, without any interests, without anything going for myself. I had been on the wrestling team the year before, but I had no friends from that. I clearly was not "one of the guys." I was an outsider and I knew it, and I couldn't fake it. I had no sense of identity and no connection to anything. I just knew that I didn't get along with people.

I was trying to be punk-rock with-out knowing what it was. I just knew it existed and I wanted it to become my thing. So I spiked my hair, and it sounds funny now, but in 1984 that was a radi-cal thing to do. The punk-rock guys at school noticed me and confronted me in the hallway. They were all older, and they said, "What's your deal? Are you punk-rock or not?" I tried to tell them that I was, and they called me out and asked me my favorite bands. It came out that I didn't know anything, and I was hanging my head. I had failed the test. They were going to reject me.

But Keith Hartell, the leader of the group, knew this was an important moment in my life. "OK," he said, "that's cool. Come with us." After school, I went over to his house, and he shaved my head and made me a mixed tape of the most important music I'd ever heard. His room was the center of the scene. He had *Maximum RocknRoll* and *Flipside*, and he told me I had to get a skateboard. All the punks had skateboards, mostly for transportation.

I started skating in September 1984 but didn't get my first board until Christmas of that year. I recognized when I started skateboarding that this was what I was going to do with the rest of my life. This was who I was. The punks didn't really skate, so I also started hanging out with these other younger guys because they skated every day after school. These weren't the punks, they were younger eighth-grade kids, and I basically ran behind them and waited until one sat down, and then I'd ask to use his board.

THEY TREATED ME LIKE A CLOWN, SO I STARTED ACT- ING CRAZY — DOING DARES, EATING STUFF — TO GET ATTENTION.

They treated me so bad—I was like a joke to them. I was older. I was weirder. They weren't misfits or outsiders. They played baseball and had the best BMX bikes and had then gotten into skating. They started abusing me, but I let them do it because I wanted to skate so badly. They always had money in their pockets, and they'd eat at stores. I'd ask for a bite and they'd call me "pauper."

They treated me like a clown, so I started acting crazy—doing dares, eating stuff—to get attention. That was the only way to be accepted, because they were a group of guys that I couldn't relate to but I wanted to be around them. They were really lame, but I didn't care—they had skateboards and *Thrasher* magazine.

I was jumping off stuff and falling on my head while they skated within their comfort zones. They thought I was a freak, but with every fall I was getting better. By the time I got my Jeff Phillips at Christmas, I was better than them. I'd skate to school in the morning and skate after school until dinner and then skate until I had to go to bed.

The kid I had seen carrying the Rising Sun board was Keith Hartell's younger brother, Kevin, who was a true skater. So I had a friend there, and there was another kid, Don, a punk rocker and a skater. I was singing in a band that grew out of this bunch of punkers, and eventually they said, "You're a skateboarder, you're not really a punker." They made the decision, not me.

This one guy lugged stolen parking blocks down into his basement, and we skated them there all winter. [*Pro skater*] Tom Groholski lived nearby, and we'd shovel the snow off his backyard ramp and dry it with towels.

I was fifteen in 1985, when we moved from New Jersey to Virginia Beach, which actually had a skate scene. I'd seen its public vert ramp, Mt. Trashmore, in the Powell Peralta video *Future Primitive*. I wore a Lance Mountain T-shirt to school on my first day. Lance has always been my favorite skater. He made skateboarding feel totally accessible, like you could *be* Lance

Mountain and have fun. Trashmore was a scene, and I'd skate with guys like Sergie Ventura, say hello, but I wasn't "friends" with them.

Then the Virginia Beach pro contest happened. Anybody who was anybody was there. I watched the pros skate vert and skated with the locals in the parking lot. I did a sad ho-ho plant in that session, and they were like, "What the hell?" A lot of people hadn't seen that trick before.

I heard clapping from the vert ramp and looked up and saw Neil Blender. He was pointing at me, saying I was amazing. He walked down with the G&S team, and they asked me where I had learned my tricks and why was I doing them the way I did.

"What's the big deal?" I asked. "Aren't the guys in Dogtown doing this stuff?" I thought Dogtown was the center of the skating universe.

"I've never seen anybody do this stuff," said Blender.

That's when it started to feel crazy. Early the next day, I was walking to 17th Street skate shop with a friend. This car pulled up, and Sergie Ventura said, "That's the guy—that's him!" And Lance Mountain gets out of the driver's seat. Holy shit…Lance Mountain. Just seeing him in person, seeing his face up close. I froze.

Lance came up to me and asked if I was the guy Blender had been talking about. "You do the handplants on both hands?" He asked me to show him some tricks, and I went through my repertoire: wallride ho-hos, triple kickflips. I started doing a demo.

Lance was giggling. "OK, I get the picture. But how are you doing those tricks on *that* board?"

My board was in ruins—no tail, trashed. He pulled out a setup from his car. "You need this more than me," he said, and drove off.

Later, at the contest, Mark Gonzales was skating in the parking lot and drawing a crowd. Gonz was flexing, putting on a show. I couldn't just be a spectator anymore. I had to skate too. Afterward, [*pro skater*] Steve Rocco skated up to me and said, "You'll never be as good as the Gonz."

People thought I was out to prove something. But then Lance and Stacy Peralta and Steve Caballero approached me. I thanked Lance for the board and he said, "You want some more? Do you want to ride for Powell Peralta?"

That night I went out to Red Lobster with Lance and Cab—suddenly I was like one of the boys. To me, Red Lobster was as high-quality as eating got, and they were just going there casually. They said I could order whatever I wanted, and nobody ever said that to me. I thought they were rich.

Daewon Song takes his role as a skater who inspires seriously. When a fan approaches, he makes eye contact and engages in a way that makes the kid love skating even more. Like his close friend Rodney Mullen, Daewon eschews the ego-stroking, materialistic side of the industry. He rides with his old nonpro friends and gravitates toward the low-key skate-rat atmosphere that first lured him into skating as a teenager.

Daewon often seeks out the fringe aspects of skating that the cool crowd ignores: Manuals, flatland, mini ramp — whatever and whenever, it's all skating to him. Apparently a lot of skaters approve of his choices — Daewon collected *Transworld*'s Street Skater of the Year in 2005 and Video Part of the Year in 2006. *Thrasher* named him its Skater of the Year in 2006.

Daewon Song, crailslide, L.A. County, 2006. **Photo:** Courtesy of Dwindle Dist.

DS: I was almost fourteen the first time I had a skateboard, in '88. I never really saw skateboarding. Where I lived in Gardena, it was more about gangbanging and tagging—those things were popular. My mom bought me a Gemco skateboard, the equivalent of a Wal-Mart board. I never really knew what it was, and my thing was just rolling on my knees, because I thought of it as transportation.

Then I met some people who actually rode "pro" boards. I remember thinking, What are pros—guys who go really fast? For years, I did not know what an ollie was.

I finally got a decent hand-me-down deck and my own launch ramp, which we called the Wrong Way Ramp. The lip at the bottom was broken, so we put a wrong-way sign on it. Suddenly I had a popular ramp, and people would knock on my door at random times and ask to skate it.

I ended up quitting skating and got jumped into an actual gang for about seven months. Some people don't have family, and they find people who have their back in gangs, but for me it was stupid. Dudes were getting killed. There was a crazy fight after school between the Dogtown Stoners and G13 versus this Crips gang. We met in a park, and dudes were getting hit in the head with two-by-fours. My friend Rob was bleeding out of his ear; there were dudes with wrecked faces. I just thought, *What am I doing?*

Throughout my life, all these wrong things I was involved with brought me back to skateboarding and made it mean more. I needed an outlet, and what activity is there that's better than skateboarding that you can do by yourself? I don't need another guy to throw a ball at me so I can catch it.

I started skating again in '90, when I was sixteen. Around that time, I got sponsored by the local shop and entered contests. All I wanted to do was eat and skate. Skating gave me a weird sense of control. It was my thing—I was going to do it when I wanted and how I wanted. Even today, the feeling I get when learning something new is the equivalent of winning the lottery.

BUT SKATING WAS DEAD AT THE TIME, AND I WAS INTO IT SO HARDCORE THAT THE FEW OTHER SKATERS THOUGHT I WAS A WEIRDO.

I didn't hang out with nonskaters. I had a few crushes in school, but skating always came first. I didn't have a serious girlfriend until I was almost nineteen. It would have changed everything if I had been involved with a girl and was busy trying to go to the Sadie Hawkins Valentine's Dance. I didn't want to dress up and go to dances—I wanted to skate.

But skating was dead at the time, and I was into it so hardcore that the few other skaters thought I was a weirdo. I'd skate to places outside my area, because I wanted to skate with guys who were better than me. I lived in Gardena but I'd skate to Carson [*seven* miles away]. I'd skate to Hermosa Beach [*eight miles*] on weekends and meet skaters. I usually only had a few bucks, not enough money for the bus and to eat, so I'd just skate and save it for a burrito for lunch. I'd meet up with this group of skaters, and we'd skate, but then they'd drive off to another spot and leave me, saying there wasn't room in the car. Maybe I was too pumped and scared them off. It was sort of weird.

For a time, my parents hated on skateboarding. It was a dead-end activity that wouldn't lead to a good job. Sometimes I had to take a test to earn my skate time.

This is a big regret—I stole from my parents. My dad had his own Shell station in South Central but he didn't want me working there because he got shot in the face at work. I had no money and was desperate for boards. One time I got caught stealing and I didn't use the money for skateboards, I bought the Garbage Pail Kids cards. I blew fifty bucks for the whole series—Messy Tessie, Ali Gator. My dad had wads of money, and I thought he wasn't going to miss fifty bucks. He missed it.

I was always skating, and some local school had a bump to a fire hydrant, and that's where Rodney [*Mullen*] first saw me skate in 1990. I didn't talk to him that first time, because he was freestyling in the tennis courts. Then he was *roommmm!*—out of there in his Camaro.

Two weeks later, I went to 135th School and saw Rodney again and skated with him. Rodney liked my skating and started sending me SMA Rocco Division boards—this was before the name was changed to World Industries.

At first my dad didn't believe I was getting the boards for free. He thought I was stealing money from him again.

Jamie Thomas took a twisting route from the Alabama backwoods to become one of the gnarliest street skaters ever. All the hurdles and prejudices and difficulties refined his determination and focus until, by 1997, he was staring down frightening skating like the Leap of Faith, a gap ollie that crushed the leg of the skater who tried it after Jamie.

When he started Zero skateboards in 1996, Jamie created a company that captured skateboarders' designated social status. A decade later, that underdog symbol is one of the most popular brands in skating, and Jamie, who helped elevate street skating, continues to inspire.

Jamie Thomas, pondering Leap of Faith, 1997. **Photo:** Grant Brittain

JT: In 1984, I was in fourth grade, and I found a red-and-yellow fiberglass skateboard with flowers on it in the attic. That was the first skateboard I'd ever seen in my life. It was my older sister's board from the '70s, and I tried to ride it in the driveway. When my sister visited, she showed me a few '70s-style freestyle moves, like walk the dog.

Two years later, I got my first decent board. My family and I had moved to Florida from Alabama, and I bought an early-'80s Sims board from my older brother's friend for twenty bucks. My brother and I stripped it, varnished it, and made it new again.

When I got to junior high, skateboarding was exploding—it seemed like everyone skated. I had a good board by then, and everyone gathered on Friday nights at this church for Skate Night. Skateboarding was heavily influenced by the punk scene at the time, and my friends and I started getting into the music of the Misfits, Dead Kennedys, and Black Flag. It felt so raw and real, like I could finally be myself.

In the middle of seventh grade, my parents decided to move back to Alabama from Florida. I knew there was no skating going on there and school in Alabama was exactly as I'd anticipated—a bunch of closed-minded rednecks. I had bangs past my chin and long shorts, and everyone in my school was like, "Who is this freak?" I started missing school regularly and got deeper into punk-rock music. I knew a few other skaters, but they lived across town and none of us had cars, so I rarely saw them. I skated by myself for what seemed like a long time.

I met some dudes that rode BMX, and it seemed kind of similar to skating 'cause you could do it wherever you wanted, so I got a bike and started racing. At the end of '88, when I was thirteen and at the bike track, these dudes were skating a launch ramp. I was like, *Yes! Now I have someone to skate with!* I introduced myself and soon we had a small scene of twenty or thirty people.

My dad is a nuclear engineer, and he wanted me to be an engineer. I took some vocational courses in electronics and basic engineering but wasn't really feeling organized education. I wanted to follow my dreams and be a pro skateboarder, but that didn't seem really realistic to him. I would always cut all my friends' hair, so I thought I could cut hair for a living or, since I knew about basic electronics, I could repair TVs if a skateboard career didn't take off.

At fifteen I started entering contests, and I placed in most and even won a few. I got a shop sponsor and then started to work at the shop. I called Real to buy boards for the shop and asked if they had any opportunities for co-sponsorship. They started flowing me the odd board and told me to send a video so they could see me skate. I sent them a video *every* month for a year and a half. The sales rep would say, "Oh, dude, the video was cool—thanks! But…you might want to use less slow-mo in the next one. I gave it to the team manager, and he wouldn't watch it." One of my videos had eighteen minutes of slow-motion skating.

Kris Markovich, who lived about two hours from where I lived, had gone to California and turned pro, which was incredibly inspiring. Around a year and a half later, he had his *Transworld* interview. I remember walking out of a skate shop with the mag and seeing his picture, and it had such an impact on me that I had to sit down on a curb: *This dude was here, and now he's in California doing it.* He had broken down the barriers from the South to California.

The skate shop went out of business, and at seventeen I quit high school and got a job at Burger King to start saving to move to California. I bought an Isuzu iMark and moved to Atlanta for the summer. I hooked up with two other skaters and we all worked telemarketing. The three of us managed to save $1,000 each. Then, right before we left, my timing belt broke, and the repair left us with $300 each.

I thought that Real, which was still flowing me boards, might help me get started in California. But when I got to San Francisco, I realized that my skating was much different from what was going on there. My gear was off, and I had outdated tricks—my Alabama version of skateboarding was odd at best.

The vibes from most of the locals were really harsh. I had no idea it would be like that, like the worst of high school. In Alabama, every skater embraced every other skater just because they rode a skateboard. If you saw somebody rolling down the street and didn't know them, you'd invite them to skate your launch ramp or whatever. At Embarcadero, I saw all the bad things I hated about high school happening to skateboarding. It almost brought me to tears at times. I remember thinking, *This isn't skateboarding, this isn't what it's supposed to be like.*

But Jim Thiebaud at Real was super-nice and said, "I can give you stuff, but I'm not sure we have a place for you." He was really encouraging, but straight with me. Thunder and Spitfire fully sponsored me, but Jim continued to go out of his way to help me out.

My two friends and I lived on the street for almost four months in San Francisco. It was fun, just like camping, except on concrete. We did catch some illnesses and had to visit the free clinic. I started putting myself on the line, doing things like jumping down Wallenberg. I wanted to make my presence known, but after six months, Jim said, "I can continue to give you boards, but I want to be straightforward—you don't have a future with Real."

I thanked him for his honesty. He was really, really cool. Obviously, he had heard from other Real riders that they thought I was a kook and shouldn't be representing their brand, but Jim still gave me stuff, and that helped keep me going. Back then I couldn't understand how rad that was. I understand it now, owning a company. I'm surprised Jim didn't spray-paint over the graphics before giving me boards. I might have done that.

I considered going home. I thought, I'm comfortable in Alabama—I'll just have to make it work. But after obsessing about the decision, I had this epiphany: *I'm here, and this is my new life, and I'm going to make something out of it. If those guys don't want to talk to me, then screw it, I won't talk to them.* I focused on having fun and skateboarding with the people who were cool to me. The situation became a positive and fueled my fire. I realized that you have to make skateboarding what it is for you and not let anyone else control that.

Growing up in Brazil, far from the peer pressure of the skateboard industry, **Bob Burnquist** took his skating in whatever direction interested him. His debut pro run at the 1995 Vancouver Slam City Jam left many a pro's mouth agape. It wasn't that he was shockingly good, it was that he was different. He did half his run switch at a time when the top pros were struggling with a single switch trick, and he won easily—both the contest and a following of the world's elite pros.

Bob's creativity and refusal to be boxed also leads him to design Dali-esque backyard skate structures, such as his corkscrew ramp. After Slam City, *Transworld Skateboarding* magazine ran a piece entitled "What About Bob?" and even though people are well aware of him, that question remains in the minds of many.

BB: I was living in São Paulo, Brazil, in the mid-'80s, and all of a sudden there was a skateboard fever. I was ten. A buddy of mine lost my soccer ball, so he gave me his old fiberglass skateboard. I took it home and cruised around on the carpet in my house.

It was more of a toy to me, but it immediately took all my attention and energy compared to everything else I did where I interacted with other people. I was small for my age and had asthma and couldn't run that much, so I was always put in goal on the school soccer team. Actually, I was a reserve goalie, so I never played. We went through a whole tournament and won and I never touched the ball. They were giving out the gold medals, and I wouldn't let them put it around my neck.

IF I SLAMMED AND PEOPLE LAUGHED, IT HAD NOTHING TO DO WITH ANYBODY ELSE.

The creative aspect of skating, going out and doing whatever I wanted, attracted me. Skating gave me that outlet. If I slammed and people laughed, it had nothing to do with anybody else. If I landed a trick and you high-fived me, you were stoked on what I did; you weren't high-fiving a team.

My parents were separated, and for my eleventh birthday, my dad bought me a board. Four months later, a private skatepark opened three blocks from my house. It had a vert ramp, a spine

mini, and street setups, and cost fifty cents a day. We'd play this game at the skatepark where we said we were Steve Caballero or Tony Hawk and fake that we were those skaters. Everyone would say who they were pretending to be, and it'd get around to me and I'd say, "I'm Bob!" I did not want to be anybody else. I was playing the game, but I was faking being a pro skater.

Pretty much from the start, I had to learn a trick every day, even if it was a little slide or some variation. When I ran out of tricks, I started doing tricks switch. I knew how to do a fakie hangup, so I just turned my body a bit and saw what worked. It was like learning how to skate all over again.

When I was sixteen, I got a Brazilian board sponsor. In '93 I went to a series of international contests in Europe, but I broke my foot the day I got there. The next year, Jake [*Phelps, editor of Thrasher*] and [*John*] Cardiel and Julian [*Stranger*] came to Brazil. I met them at a park and could speak English, and I took them to spots. I was a dirty skateboarder with these ragged jeans I wore every day and my sweaty baseball hat. I skated with them and did a switch frontside ollie over the channel, and 540s. They were stoked and gave me a setup, and Jake said, "You have to go to the U.S.—people have no idea what you're doing." I was stoked: Jake was full-on. The guy is a skateboarder.

In the summer of '94, I went to the U.S. and stayed in San Francisco and started getting boards from Real. I wanted to leave high school early in 1995 to skate in the U.S., and told my mom that I'd do this [*early exit*] method of graduating. You had to finish

120 tests, and I got through 80 of them when it was time for Slam City Jam in Vancouver.

I had no expectations at the Slam City Jam. I was eighteen, and it was my first pro contest, and nobody knew who I was. Jake was on the platform and asked if I could drop into a 540, and I did. He was almost coaching me in a way—not to "win" but to make a first impression. He helped me put a run together: "Make sure you throw the switch stuff in there."

I bailed both my prelim runs and ran back up and did the rest of the run switch. The announcer was freaking out, but I didn't think I'd make the finals. I was surprised that people were so into it. I put my finals run together and was stoked, and then they started calling out the results. When they got to the top two, they asked [*Mike*] Frazier and me to come up. I was stoked—second place! Then they announced that Frazier had second. I was completely dumbfounded.

I moved out to the U.S. with my sister shortly after, and I did get my high school diploma at City College in San Francisco.

Armed with a wide smile, hippie hair, creative facial foliage, and a bag of imaginative tricks, **Chris Haslam** has a talent for making his skating inclusive as well as awe-inspiring. You get the vibe that he would still have fun skating with you even if you straight-up sucked. And you'd be right — the bearded one has been spotted playing games of SKATE with ten-year-old local rats at his home skatepark in Richmond, British Columbia. Haslam always seems to find a way to see the radness in any-body's skating.

Some pros make you want to mimic their tricks, and others make you want to duplicate the feeling they get from skating. Haslam does both. His 2005 *Transworld* readers' poll win for Favorite Skater was a landslide — almost double the number of votes as the runner-up.

Chris Haslam, pole 'n' roll, L.A. County, 2006. **Photo:** Courtesy of Dwindle Dist.

CH: I moved to Bukit Timah, Singapore, in '91, when I was eleven, and I'd always see this French guy skating around my area of town, and it looked fun. In '93 I got my first real board for Christmas, a Santa Cruz, and my older brother got a slick Real board. A deck alone in Singapore cost around eighty bucks, pretty expensive. I started hanging out at Go Sports, a local skate shop—there were only two in all of Singapore at the time. We'd hang out with a whole group of dudes. The odd dude from Scotland stationed nearby on a navy ship would come down and skate. He might be able to do 360 flips, and that would influence everybody for a little while. We'd watch videos, but they were delayed, sometimes a whole year off, and you had to have a universal VCR, because it was a different format.

We'd skate at the McDonald's drive-through, the stairs at the building where my mom worked, some marble ledges downtown—sick spots. Bukit Timah also had a nature park with gnarly monkeys. They'd steal your bag if you left it out, take your camera. Sometimes we'd provoke them a little too much and end up running down the hill with ten monkeys chasing us. Their teeth are huge.

Being in Singapore and away from the industry kept skating fun for me. I wasn't thinking about getting sponsored, except as some sort of "wouldn't it be cool…" fantasy. I was a kid going to school, and being so far away shaped my sense of skating.

In '96, when I was sixteen, my older brother and I moved back to London, Ontario. My dad paid for an apartment and school, and gave us 200 bucks a month. We had to take care of the rest.

We were pure skate rats. It was awesome. We found BB guns and shot at each other in the apartment. A friend had a Petro Canada card, and we'd load up on junk food from the gas station.

I HAD RAGGEDY, WORN-OUT SHOES AND HAD TO PUT PLASTIC PHONE CARDS BETWEEN THE INSOLE AND SOLE TO PROTECT MY FEET.

In '97, I went back to Singapore to live, and they'd built a skatepark. It was a brutal park. The worst. All wood, some bars, launch ramps, a six-foot mini ramp with two feet of vert. But it was a scene, and all the skaters knew each other. We skated it every day, all day. Later that year, my parents moved to Richmond, British Columbia. I was skating and going to college. Since I was moving around so much, skating was the only constant in my life—it was always there for me. It's a form of expression.

I had raggedy, worn-out shoes and had to put plastic phone cards between the insole and sole to protect my feet. All my clothes were from my dad, who is a professor—when he visited a university and they gave him a football T-shirt or something, he would give it to me. I wore the most random gear—I looked pretty harsh, but I wasn't fussy.

I had these tearaway pants, and all the buttons ripped off the sides so I laced shoelaces through the holes to keep them together.

I didn't know any other skaters in Richmond and just skated in this area in front of my house. Luckily, three months after I moved, they built an outdoor skatepark across the street from my house. I went there every day and met my buddy Steve, and I've been skating with him ever since. My group of friends was pretty small, and I still had the Singapore mentality. I never went to downtown Vancouver to skate. I was having fun at the skatepark by my house.

I met John Remondo, who owned this Richmond skate shop, the Boarding House. It was the best shop ever, and my first sponsor, from '99 until they closed in 2001. The guys who ran the shop weren't into skating to make money; you could tell they loved skating. They had this awesome giant grip-tape ball made out of scraps. That shop influenced me a lot. I've never had another shop sponsor, because the Boarding House was the sickest one I could ever have.

Through the Boarding House, I got introduced to the guys at Ultimate Skateboards Distribution. I was twenty years old, and I didn't think anything was going to happen with major sponsorship. I had made some small sponsor-me videos, but nothing ever happened—no companies had even replied. Steve just filmed me, and it was shot like an episode of *Cops*, all shaky. Sponsor Land sucked, and I was over it.

Then Kelly Jablonski, [*the general manager*] from Ultimate, asked me for another sponsor-me video. Daewon [*Song*] saw the video, and a month later I was flying down to California to skate with him as a sort of audition. It happened so fast that I was tripping out. I skated with him in a warehouse until two in the morning, and Rodney [*Mullen*] walked in. I was like, *Holy shit!* I didn't know what to say to him. He watched me skate and put me on Tensor, and I got on Deca that day, too.

All these thoughts about skating with my friends in Singapore—and never thinking of getting sponsored—went through my head. I was tripping out.

PRO
SKATER

FOR SKATERS, THE DEFINITION OF THE TERM "PRO-FESSIONAL" IS LOOSE. Does it describe a person with a professional skateboard model? There are X Games competitors sans board sponsors. Is it someone who enters pro contests? There are pros with megaselling boards who haven't competed in years.

There needs to be a label, and the one that stuck is unfortunately the same one traditional sports employ. That's why, when Tony Hawk "retired" from competition, the mainstream press covered the news as if he were hanging up his skateboard and moving to a golf course in Florida. They assumed that no competition meant no "professional" label.

There has never been a strict job description for a professional skateboarder. It basically boils down to a skater possessing something that makes people want to emulate him enough to buy his product. Because skating is a culture as well as an activity, a popular pro needs personality as well as skills on a board. Then again, anybody can turn pro—you could right now, with a stack of blanks and a screenprinter.

Mike Vallely, boneless, School W, 1986. **Photo:** Grant Brittain

THERE WAS NO SUCH THING AS A PROFESSIONAL SKATEBOARDER

Stacy Peralta: Russ Howell might have been one of the only skaters to get paid at the time [1975]. I know he was the first skateboarder to get a [*mainstream*] deal with Grentec. He even did TV commercials back then. But there was no such thing as a professional skateboarder as it's understood today.

AS FAR AS I KNOW, I WAS THE FIRST PRO SKATER

Russ Howell: In the early '60s, they used established surf stars to promote skateboarding. Skateboarding never had any big stars of its own until 1975.

My first skateboard contest in Huntington Beach in 1975 awarded me a ten-speed bike. The April 1975 Del Mar contest gave away trophies only. A contest in South Bay in July 1975 gave a motorcycle to the first-place winner. I think '76 was the first year a contest awarded money.

As far as I know, I was the first pro skater. After the '75 Del Mar Nationals contest, skateboarding really exploded. I was twenty-five, the old guy in the sport. When I began winning other contests, companies started saying, "If this guy is winning the contest, he'd be a good spearhead for promoting the sport. We can put him on an airplane and send him anywhere in the world without a chaperone." I had three sponsors my first year, and then the next year 150 people were paying me for doing demos, product endorsements, TV shows, and commercials. A professional skater's contest winnings may amount to only a few thousand dollars, a fraction of his total income.

I THINK I WAS BORN WITH A MUSTACHE. I CAN'T EVER REMEMBER BEING WITHOUT ONE.

Skateboard organizations, such as the United States Skateboard Association in 1975 and the International Skateboard Association in 1976, began to develop rules for competition and for amateur and pro divisions.

There were people who really hurt the sport in the '70s. There were two factions during that time, no doubt about it. There was a line drawn, and everybody knew it. You were either going to be a druggie and say, "I really shred and tear, and I'm a badass." Or you were going to say, "You know what? I'm just going to try and do something for the sport. I want to gain some sponsorships, and I want big contests, and I want people to feel that this is a professional sport."

I was a physical-education major, and I wanted to help integrate skateboarding into public school athletics and into a place where the International Olympic Committee would consider it a sport. There were a lot of skaters who did not like my approach and didn't want me in the sport, I've got to admit. I don't think age played into it—I was just stealing the limelight from other people. The Dogtown skaters said, "We don't want this organized stuff! We just want to thrash!" I was not profit-oriented. Consider this: I come in to the Del Mar National, and I take first place. There is no profit to be made there.

Being sponsored by Grentec turned out to be an enormous mistake. They linked me with their stupid little cheap boards. It was an embarrassment. I could see why other skaters thought I had sold out. I was supposed to get $2,000 a month and a percentage of sales of a high-end professional model that was never manufactured. I never saw a dime off of that contract.

I got away from Grentec after a year and went to work with Innovate Design. I was with them for two years and never saw a dime off of that, either. I was an idiot. The owner finally went to jail. I got so burned out that I moved to Australia for six months after receiving an invitation to organize provincial skate contests.

Stacy Peralta: Russ [Howell] didn't have youth on his side. He was in his early twenties, and we were sixteen, seventeen years old. We had long blond hair and we looked like rats, and Russ looked like a professional athlete. Russ was an amazing skateboarder, but he was an older guy and resembled more of a guy out of the '60s in his look and his skateboarding. We resembled what was new, which was far more aggressive.

Russ Howell: I think I was born with a mustache. I can't ever remember being without one.

I THOUGHT I WAS GOING TO BE A PLUMBER

Stacy Peralta: The original Zep skate team broke up in '76, but about five of us were still left on it. The other guys went to E-Z, where Jay [Adams]'s father made the boards. We all showed up at a contest on two different teams. And then right after that, when I was probably seventeen years old, I went to Australia as one of the first skateboarders to introduce it there. I didn't get paid anything from that trip. They didn't offer me anything, and I didn't ask. They just covered expenses, and I was excited to go.

When I got back, the Zephyr shop was closing. G&S offered me a phenomenal deal: four different skateboard models and a really fair royalty. If I didn't have the best deal, I had one of the best deals in skateboarding. I was making $4,000, $5,000 a month—a lot of money at the time, more than my parents were making.

The thing that was unusual about G&S, as opposed to all the other skateboard companies, was that they actually ran their business properly. If they said, "We're going to make 6,000 to 10,000 skateboards a month, and we're going to sell that many," they did it. I got fifty cents a board.

You had mainstream companies like Grentec, but the only other ones you had were surf companies. Unity Skateboards, which Ty Page rode for, was a surf shop. Most other skateboard companies were run by young surfers who didn't really know what they were doing. Some were run by guys trying to turn their pot businesses into legitimate businesses, and a lot of skateboarders got caught up with those guys.

Professional skateboarding meant that I could quit my restaurant job and junior-college classes. I thought I was going to be a plumber. I wasn't aware that I had a lot of capabilities until skateboarding came along.

But there was still no idea of where it would lead. People thought, *You'll ride this wave, and when it's done you'll go sell cars or be an insurance-policy salesman.* We were on the leading edge. And in a sense we still are—I never thought that in my late forties, I'd be skating bowls and pools.

I HAD RUN AWAY FROM HOME TO BECOME A PROFESSIONAL SKATEBOARDER

Dave Hackett: After winning the Hang Ten contest in 1975 without a sponsor, I thought I'd better get good quick, because sponsors were the key to getting places. Back then, most of the best skaters were underage, and the sponsors were like a second set of parents.

Shortly after, photographer Ray Allen told Dave Macintyre at Gordon & Smith that I was pretty hot and had won a few contests, that I was the next Alva and did these airs and all this other stuff. G&S sponsored me as an amateur.

G&S was really organized, which was kind of difficult for me, because I didn't fit into that team thing. I had to wear these stupid team shirts, and it was just fucked. I liked the people running it, though. Stacy [*Peralta*] was in a whole other realm. He was definitely the most popular skater at the time, along with Alva. G&S owned the market with Bahne in the late '70s. They made great products, but I felt as if I had sold out to the milk-and-toast factory.

They more or less had a sit-down talk with me and said, "You can't be acting like one of these Dogtown guys. You're on G&S now and we're a Christ-centered company, and we can't be taking you around if this is what you're going to be doing." They were cool—they were just saying what their deal was, and it wasn't my deal.

I finally got kicked off the team after a year and a half for destroying a hotel room. I got kicked off many teams for being an obnoxious little asshole. In 1978, Alva Skates took me to Florida for the U.S. Open men's pool or bowl thing, and I won the event.

Being *pro* back then meant that you were basically competing against guys who were men—guys in their twenties, even late twenties. It was an age thing. You only made money if you won. There weren't a lot of pro models. Stacy had one, Ray Bones had one, Henry Hester had a pro slalom board, Alva had his board. But turning pro didn't translate into making money. Even though I won the pool contest, I still was not going to get a model from Alva Skates. I didn't even care, in a way—it wasn't a make-or-break deal. That really wasn't how you made money. What I really wanted was a monthly salary, to stay in skating and make the most money possible. A lot of the time we would just get as much equipment as possible from our sponsors and sell it or trade it for weed or blow.

I had run away from home to become a professional skateboarder. It was the only thing I dreamed about. I left home and didn't return for two years. I had no contact with my parents. I was seventeen and I walked out of school. I was over it. I didn't even clean out my locker, just walked right by it. Never went back to school,

1

3

2

1 **Steve Olson**, first pool champion, 1978. **Photo:** James Cassimus
2 **Russ Howell**, mustache, 1976. **Photo:** Courtesy of Russ Howell
3 **Dave Hackett**, Velcro board backside ollie, L.A. football game, 1978. **Photo:** James Cassimus

never showed up at my parents' house again. I went to Kent Senator's house—he was a pro skateboarder who rode for Turning Point. His brother had the Turning Point ramp, which was the capsule [*seen in the movie* Skateboard Madness].

Kent and I had just cut a deal to go to England for Arrow Skateboards/Tracknology wheels. We had two weeks until we left. The month before, when I had gone to Florida and won the U.S. Open, this eccentric English billionaire guy who owned an injection molding company had contacted me. He said, "I'm putting together the best skateboard team in the world. I want ten of the hottest guys in the world. Interested?"

"What does it pay?"

"We're paying everybody the same—three hundred dollars a day." *Per day.* That's like nine grand a month. You know how much money that was in 1978?

"And," he continued, "I'll buy you your own car, and you'll have your own place. You'll stay with me at first, but you guys have to move to England, because that's where we're going to make a go of it." The guy owned a castle in Coventry with a fifteen-person staff.

We hit pay dirt. Bobby Piercy, Tony [*Alva*], Jay [*Adams*], Kent [*Senator*], Jerry Valdez, Shogo [*Kubo*], Paul Constantineau—these are the guys who went to England, except for Alva, who backed out at the last minute.

My parents said, "You're not doing that! You're going to stay in school and get an education."

"WE'RE PAYING EVERYBODY THE SAME— THREE HUNDRED DOLLARS A DAY." *PER DAY.* THAT'S LIKE NINE GRAND A MONTH. YOU KNOW HOW MUCH MONEY THAT WAS IN 1978?

That's when I knew—I'm going to England. I don't care what it takes, if I have to run away from home and quit school…and that's what I did.

My job was to skate pro and be part of the design team. We designed skateboard parks and products for the company. We ended up building three skateboard parks. The guy had an aircraft hangar, and he built us a perfect six-foot-high halfpipe inside. It had no flat bottom—it was a solid U—but it was 100 feet long. I skated that every day.

I was in England for about nine months, making three hundred bucks a day. I didn't save any of it. We spent it on hookers, three-piece tailored suits. We all had brand-new cars. I had a white BMW 2002tii…it was probably the most ultimate skate trip *ever*. We eventually got deported from England for lewd and lascivious behavior. The things that people pay to see on *Jackass*, we were doing back then and getting arrested for.

I came back and lived down in San Diego for about a year. The pay switched to a couple thousand dollars a month, and then it dwindled down into nothing. In 1979, I really needed to win the Oasis contest for the 1,500 bucks in prize money.

I finally went home to Malibu and talked to my parents. My mom wanted to scratch my eyes out. She threw the six-foot-tall U.S. Open trophy at me. It shattered into a million pieces. The only piece I have of it is a part of the plaque that says first place. My mom was clinically ill, chemically off-balance. Back then they didn't diagnose stuff like that. If they had, she and my brother would probably still be alive and on meds. But that's another story.

I WILL BE COOL TO KIDS

Steve Olson: One time [in 1977], before I was even sponsored, I was skating the Fruit Bowl with my friend. There was this big session with Warren Bolster [editor of SkateBoarder], some of the Dogtown and San Diego dudes, and Waldo Autry, Wally Inouye—all these cats, all the big dudes. They went to this new skatepark, Concrete Wave. We were outside the fence watching these dudes, and I remember telling my friend, "These assholes might be able to skateboard, but they certainly can't surf." They were dicks to us. Not every one, but there was a definite separation. I thought, If I'm ever in that position, I will be cool to kids.

My pro model came out somewhere in '78. And then wide boards came out in around the third pro pool contest in Newark. I never saw royalties. I still got my salary. I have no idea. I couldn't have cared less. I was so stoked on life that it was frightening.

I got [SkateBoarder's] Skater of the Year that same year. Fuck no, I wasn't expecting that. At that point I was totally into punk rock, and a lot of skateboarders were lame. I was isolated inside skating. I'd go to contests and be smoking these dudes, and they would still call me a faggot. I took on an elitist attitude: OK, you guys don't get it. You call me gay because I have my ear pierced and I cut my hair short when everybody else has theirs long, and I wear tight clothes and whatever. It was totally excellent. Halloween was every day, and the music was sick.

I remember exactly what I wore to the awards ceremony. I had a white dinner jacket, like James Bond. My friends from TSOL had broken into a bondage-sex shop and stolen all this shit, and I was wearing leather pants they'd given me. I had little pointy black-and-white shoes and a polka-dotted tie and a black shirt, and my hair was cut short. Alva was into it—his art-department dudes were totally down and turned him on to it.

They announced the reader's poll awards at this formal dinner. The older guys were there, the controllers of the industry. We were the kids. They announced who-ever got third, and Alva got second. I was like, Fuck, I didn't make the top twenty— what a joke. I had just won the overall at the Henry Hester series.

And then they called me up and said I'd won and yelled, "Speech! Speech!" I was totally hyped out of my mind. I couldn't believe it. I was obviously over-whelmed. By then, Alva had thrown his runner-up trophy in the trash as he walked away, because he hadn't won again. He had been looking for a two-year sweep. I was just a punk-ass kid, influenced by the punks around the world, so I spat at a couple of cameras and picked my nose and flicked boogers and refused to say anything. That freaked the industry out. The two top dogs in that little world were rebelling against their establishment. *Pow!*—it just blew up: "These guys aren't good for skateboarding…bad representation." One skater guy wrote to the magazine, something about how skateboarding was in a bad place with Alva and me as the top guys.

I went to Michigan in '79 for a demo or something with my hair dyed blond. I went to the skatepark before all the other pro dudes. I was skating, and these kids were anticipating the pros to roll up, but I had blond hair, so they didn't recognize me. These two little punk kids said, "You're pretty good."

I was like, "Yeah, whatever." I was just skating around and talking to them. I was around seventeen, and these kids were maybe three years younger.

They said, "Whoa, you're really good! You know, these pro dudes from California are coming here today."

"Really? Are they good?"

"Yeah! They're the best!"

Then [*Brad*] Bowman, Bert LaMar, T.A., and all these dudes roll up and say, "Hey, what's up, Olson?"

The kids were all, "No way!"

I grabbed the kids and said, "If you kids treat me any other way than you did in the beginning, I'll beat your fucking ass. Let's go skate."

I DIDN'T UNDERSTAND WHY I WAS WINNING

Stacy Peralta: I was so ridiculously surprised that I won the 1979 *SkateBoarder* magazine Skater of the Year. I was taking a pee when they announced it. I didn't understand why I was winning, because my career had already crested. I can only assume that it was because I had the company [*Powell Peralta*] and because of the cool ads we did. We had the hot company and it was emerging, and maybe people thought I was happening because I had gathered this team that kicked ass. That was the last award [*of that type*]. There was no more *SkateBoarder* around after that—it went out of business.

I DON'T EVEN LIKE THIS STORY

Lance Mountain: In '79 I saw the Lakewood Pro/Am, and then I went to England. I skated the Mad Dog Bowl, and the skatepark owner's son said, "Alva was just here, and you're better than him."

I understood why he said that. Inverts had just come out, and I did them and Alva didn't. You had to learn new tricks right away. I don't even like this story, because it can be misconstrued. I never thought I was better than Alva, but I did think, *Maybe I can do what those guys did and enter contests and try to get sponsored.*

In 1980, I won almost every amateur contest. Right when I started entering pro contests, I thought, *We're going to be skating against* [Brad] *Bowman and Duane*

[Peters]! And then—*whish!* They were gone. I didn't even get to ride against the guys I looked up to. They'd stopped skating. Looking back, I realize now that we turned pro because the industry needed pros. I got on Variflex in '81, and then the whole pro team quit. The older pros dropped off, because there was no money. Companies saw the younger skaters and simply went, "You're the next pros."

IT WAS ALWAYS DEFEND, DEFEND, DEFEND

<u>Kevin Harris</u>: No matter how many contests you won in Canada in the late '70s and early '80s, you had to know somebody major in California to get a legitimate sponsor. Russ Howell and other pros would come up to emcee some contests, and you just prayed that they might say, "You're really good, you want to ride for…"

Never happened.

When Stacy [*Peralta*] sponsored me in 1983 at a contest in California, I was buzzing the whole time, but that feeling faded when I left that bubble. I'd come home from a pro contest where I'd placed in the top three, and my father-in-law would say sarcastically, "Wow, you won 100 bucks!"

In my mind, it was like, *Holy shit! I won 100 bucks—from skateboarding!* But the real world looked at it as a big joke. You're in a world-class competition and you get third, and you get 100 bucks? Aunts and uncles would ask me when did I get too old to skateboard, and if I actually made a living from it, I'd exaggerate how much I made. I was always trying to defend skateboarding. It was always defend, defend, defend. I was about to get married in the early '80s, and people assumed that Audrey would carry me financially, because she had the good job at the airline that paid fifteen bucks an hour.

My friends who used to live on skateboards were like, "Oh, you're still playing with a skateboard?" People my age would see me skate and say, "Wow, you're really good!" Then they'd throw in the negative: "Is skateboarding still even around?" It was pretty much: *OK, you're talented, but you're a loser.*

I was pro for three years before I got a board, in 1986. I was on the most popular skateboard team, Powell Peralta, and placing top three in almost every freestyle contest. I even won one, but I didn't get paid for the first three years. Powell paid only for my travel and expenses at contests, and for product. I was happy. It didn't bother me that I had to wait in line for my model. Rodney [*Mullen*] had come out with a board in '82, and Per [*Welinder*]'s was next in '84, and I was after him in '86. If we had been street or vert skaters, our boards would have come out instantly.

Was I doing the right thing? In my mind, I had to have skating. I figured that I'd make fifty bucks over here and twenty bucks over there and scrape by. I had so much pride in skating and was so determined to wake up the world and show it that skating was this amazing sport, or whatever you want to call it.

Tony Hawk, Kona skatepark, 1983. **Photo:** Grant Brittain

STALEFISH

I MUST HAVE SOLD A SINGLE BOARD THAT MONTH

Tony Hawk: In 1982 I went pro at the Whittier Turkey Shoot on Thanksgiving. I had started winning amateur contests, but it wasn't a certain skill level that made me turn pro—it was because a lot of the other amateurs I was neck-and-neck with had gone pro. I would have looked like a pussy, just playing it safe so I could win it all.

Turning pro meant you checked the "pro" box instead of the "am" box on the entry form. And you were in the running for prize money—100 bucks for first place. At the Turkey Shoot, I talked to Stacy, and he just said, "It's your decision. Whatever you feel comfortable with."

Being pro wasn't that different, because I skated against a lot of the same guys I had in the amateur circuit. The older pros were already moving out. Guys like Duane [Peters], Steve Olsen, Eddie Elguera were done with skating. They were over it, and old enough that they probably had to find a job, because no one was making a living as a pro skater. Looking back, it's funny how big I thought those events were. In my memory, it seemed like a ton of people watched, but when I look at pictures there are maybe a couple hundred, if that. And it was all people who were in the industry, or skated themselves.

I got my pro model when I was fifteen, in '83. My point standings were really good, and that was important. Even if I wasn't winning each contest, I was consistently placing high enough to win the overall [National Skateboard Association] series, which meant a lot back then.

My first royalty check was in the twenty-dollar range, but there weren't a lot of reorders, so it dropped to four dollars a month, even eighty-five cents once. I must have sold a single board that month. Eventually the checks increased slightly. My parents weren't that well-off, so I was hyped to get a check for fifty bucks. I remember putting my checks in the bank, and at some point my bank account got to 600 dollars, and that was huge. I was saving up for a car.

Being a professional skater didn't do anything for my social hierarchy at school, because I was a ghost. As soon as the bell rang, I was out of there. On weekends I was traveling to events or contests. There was no connection to my life at school. Some of my classmates knew there was a pro skater at their school, but they wouldn't have been able to pick me out of a lineup. One guy at school saw me skating and said that there was a pro skater named Tony Hawk who went to our school. I told him that was my name, and he said, "Really? Well, you don't look like that dude."

IT BECAME AN INSANE AMOUNT OF ANXIETY

Rodney Mullen: People at school knew about me being a professional skateboarder and a "world champion," and there was definite respect, but there were no rockstar [powers] that suddenly worked with the girls. Skateboarding still wasn't cool. The "world champion" was just a title, really. The trophy could have had anything on top of it. There was no skater-punk-kid prejudice from the teachers, because my grades were good. It was more like, "Can you believe he does well in school and skateboards?"

But I was socially bankrupt. Completely. I'd do all my homework during lunch so I could focus on skating after school on the tennis courts that were hidden by a hedge. I'd skate late, and on Friday nights I remember staring at the buses arriving for football games and everybody having a good time, and it sunk in—*I don't know any of these people, but I'd love to.* I'd feel lonely for a sec—*This sucks.* But then I'd think, *I have this world, and you can't have it all.*

I could skate in front of people—I had been doing that since I was a little kid. But what do you do afterward, when they're all coming at you? I can't talk to them. I'm here to skate—I can't do anything more.

It became an insane amount of anxiety. As long as I was skating, I was safe. When I was about twenty-five, I actually learned to enjoy talking to kids. You know what helped me? I got to see other pro skaters freaking out and tripping out and not knowing how to handle it. I could see that kids are kids. They're just curious.

It's a huge conflict. In some ways, you're taking the people least fit to deal with this type of attention and very quickly making them deal with it. Occasionally, there's the guy who's perfectly made for that, but it usually takes a lot of experience.

IT DIDN'T MAKE ANY SENSE THAT YOU COULD MAKE MONEY SKATEBOARDING

Tommy Guerrero: I didn't want to go pro for a long time. What was I going to go pro for exactly? There was no such thing as a "street skater" in 1983. Then I had a conversation with, of all people, Lee Cole, who runs Skates on Haight. He's this cat who everybody kind of despises, but he had some good wisdom for me: "Why *not* turn professional?" He put it in my head that street skating was actually viable within the skateboard world. Maybe it was because he was a businessperson, and he saw you could make money on it. I'm not sure. That was a turning point for me.

I had never looked at it as a way to make money. It didn't make any sense that you could make money skateboarding. It was completely ridiculous. My first pro contest was in 1985, and I was on the Powell team for a year without a pro model. I made no money from Powell, and I worked at the skate shop Concrete Jungle. I got a $500 Christmas bonus from Powell, and that was it.

I think there was a bit of dissent from the rest of the Powell team—a lot of the guys were like, "What's he pro for?" There was a "pro street skater—what's that?" sort of attitude.

There wasn't even any real skate equipment designed for what I did. I told Powell, "Your wheels are too big, it's outrageous." Those big Cubics or mini-Cubics? They were massive. I tried riding the freestyle wheels, and they were great for street, nice and hard. Then we went to the roller-skate wheels, and those became Rat Bones.

My board came out in '86. My first [royalty] check was for $3,900. That was more money than I'd made in my entire existence. Suddenly I needed to open a bank account. I was nineteen, and that was my first bank account. I didn't have a car—I didn't get my license until I was twenty-five—so it was, *What do I do with this?* I just kept putting all this money into a checking account.

CHINESE CULTURE CE

Tommy Guerrero, corner air, China Banks, 1987. **Photo:** Grant Brittain

Mike Vallely, pondering bomb drop, New York, 2001. **Photo:** Grant Brittain

STALEFISH

I was on Powell for about five years. Real was just starting in 1990 when I came aboard with Jim [*Thiebaud*]. Powell had had a bunch of new hotshoes, and just like anything, old guys were out, new kids were in. Around this time, the Powell team manager came up for one of the Frisco Disco contests, or whatever they were, and said, "We've heard some things about what you've been doing up here, partying, smoking crack," and some other shit. And they heard I wasn't skating. The next day I ended up getting second or third or something. They wanted an excuse to get rid of me for whatever reason. I was like, "All right, fine, I get the message now."

Maybe they didn't just believe in me anymore, and new kids were coming in with new tricks, and they were trying to cover their ass. I talked to Stacy [*Peralta*] before I left. To some degree, he sort of understood. I talked to Fausto [*Vitello, cofounder of Independent trucks and* Thrasher *magazine*] about it too, and he felt bad, because Real was Fausto's company and he was friends with Stacy. But Fausto knew I had to move on, and he was always there to support me.

The thing that sucked was that I appealed to Stacy's rational side: "I know what's going on—they're trying to shelve me. I know I'm becoming a dinosaur to some degree. I understand. I have to move on and do my thing, and you have kids to bring up in the ranks." But the next time I saw him he was totally cold-shoulder, when I had thought we were cool with it. That really bummed me out, because I really looked up to Stacy— he was sort of my de facto dad to some degree. Stacy took care of us. We stayed at his house all the time. He told us not to be kooks. He was not just a businessperson with us, and I definitely confided in him. But everything kind of worked out with Stacy later on.

Starting Real wasn't scary. It was surreal, if anything. I knew that I wasn't going to be an engineer or flip burgers. I dropped out of school around the tenth grade. I needed a future, and I wanted to be involved with skating.

Powell had become a massive company that was paralyzed by its size. Real was a reaction to Powell in the philosophical sense, and to what was going on in the skateboard industry. When we did demos, we had everyone skate with us. It wasn't the Pony Show with TG and Jim, it was "Let's just all skate." We tried to diminish that rock-star thing. When we did wheels, we sold them in six-packs, so if two guys bought them they could sell the extra set to a buddy and get wheels cheaper. It was tiny at the beginning—there were about four people running the company.

I had bought a condo, and at Real I made about a third of what I had made with Powell. There were times on Powell when I'd make anything from $3,000 to $10,000 a month. At Real I was making $1,500 a month. It was brutal. I had to get roommates to pay the bills. And I had to work.

I WAS IN THE HOSPITAL FOR TWO WEEKS AND HAD BLOOD TRANSFUSIONS

Mike Vallely: I was shocked when Stacy Peralta called in 1987 and said we were going to move forward with my pro model. I had just gotten on, and Powell had a tradition of waiting a long time to turn skaters pro. We started working on my board immediately, but I entered my first pro contest in the summer of 1987, when I was still sixteen.

My biggest problem that I ever had in skateboarding was that it all happened too fast. I think some people saw me as a threat. Skating was changing, and I was the face of change. It sucked for me—I didn't want to signify a change in skateboarding. I didn't want to be *that* guy. The first thing written about me in *Transworld Skateboarding* had a negative angle to it. GSD wrote about how I had no history in skateboarding, and he was one of my heroes.

Everything happened too fast. My way of dealing with and escaping the skate industry was by skating. But at a certain point, it began to affect my skating. I dropped out of school in the eleventh grade to go on the Hell Tour with Steve Rocco. I was a lot younger than my age—very naive, very sensitive—and, because I was traveling coast-to-coast for contests and demos, I'd essentially left home. Nobody ever sat me down and explained what the expectations were. I just hit these walls that I didn't know existed.

By default, Rocco stepped in as a father figure. I knew Steve wasn't the right guy, but he was there. My first pro board came out in June '87, and I left Powell the following February. I had been getting monthly royalty checks of more than $10,000, but I didn't think of leaving as a "bad career move." Why would I care if it was a bad career move? I went from being a kid who had not a cent in his pocket to buying a sports car. I flew my friends around and went on shopping sprees. I spent every penny.

I went to Steve's company and put it on the map. [*World Industries had just been started with loan-shark money, and the industry predicted a quick death until Mike joined the team.*] I had a monthly guarantee from Rocco for $5,000 a month. But I began selling more boards than that. My biggest monthly check was almost $14,000. I was renting a really expensive condo on the beach. I was with my girlfriend, Ann. I had season tickets for the Kings.

In theory, I loved what World Industries was supposed to be about: skater-run, we'd make the decisions. But Rocco made the decisions. I'd never have mocked Powell with ads. I may not have belonged on Powell, but I would never have mocked something that was so important to my life. I had a bad experience at Powell Peralta, but those videos changed my life. Regardless of what had happened between me and Stacy—he was still Stacy Peralta, and Powell Peralta was my favorite company.

I didn't have a good relationship with Rocco. I didn't really have a good relationship with my peers. Around 1989, I burned out on skateboarding. It had been turned inside out and exposed and trampled in the dirt.

But I never stopped skating. People thought I did, because I wasn't very visible in the early '90s. I was almost twenty, which is your prime for skateboarding, and I completely rejected everything and it was painful. I dealt with it by skating with Ed Templeton and not making an effort to be the best guy around. I didn't want to be the best guy—I just wanted to be me.

In 1992 I organized my own demos with Ed with no hype. We did demos across North America in strip malls, in parking lots—anywhere people would host us. I wasn't in the magazines as much, I wasn't in advertisements, but I toured.

Every summer I'd get in the van go to skate shops and skateparks. I was controlling my own career.

The ulcer was a culmination of…everything from Virginia Beach back in '86 to that moment in 1992. I was twenty-two and not making the money I was used to as a pro skater. I hadn't saved anything, and I owed the government almost $40,000 in taxes. And my wife was pregnant. The word on the street was that I was washed up. Ed and I were doing our own company with Brad Dorfman, and it was sketchy—things were spiraling out of control.

The tour ended, but Ed and I flew to New York for a few extra demos. I knew something was wrong with me. Halfway through a dinner, I had to go outside and lie down on the sidewalk. I was paralyzed. I skated a demo the next day, flew back to California, and went straight to the hospital.

I was in the hospital for two weeks and had blood transfusions. And I had no insurance. And I had a baby coming. My parents said, "OK, Mike, time to grow up and get on with your life." My wife was the one who said, "No. You're meant to do this."

IT WAS FUNNY BEING FIRED AS A PRO SKATER

Bob Burnquist: I turned pro in Brazil when I was fifteen, but it didn't mean anything outside of Brazil. After winning Slam City Jam in '95, I moved to San Francisco. I told Real that if they couldn't pay me, I could sell skate product. I'd get $5,000 worth of product from Deluxe and sell it in Brazil. I did it with a buddy about five times. Full contraband. Full gray market. After a while, Real paid me around $700 a month, and that was great, but I needed more to live.

Then Julian [Stranger] talked to me about riding for Anti-Hero. My first pro board in the U.S. was from Anti-Hero. When they came up with their logo, I was amped on the eagle and amped on the whole group, and I wanted to remember that phase of my life, so I went and got the logo tattoo. After a while, I was getting around $1,500 a month, and a couple hundred from a wheel sponsor and trucks. The perks, like free travel, were better than the pay.

It ended in '99, around five years after I got on. It was a little weird. When I won Slam City, I was automatically invited to compete in the first Extreme Games [now the X Games]. It was super-polarizing, compared to what Anti-Hero was about. But for a skater from Brazil, it was super-important to be on TV in front of all the viewers around the world. I was looking to make a living from skateboarding. I knew it was cheesy, but it was a necessary evil for me, because I wanted Brazilians to see what I was doing in the U.S. and have one of their own to be stoked on.

It was a conflict. We had a meeting and they told me I couldn't skate the X Games. I said, "Um, I'm a skateboarder—I can do whatever I want. You can't tell me I can't skate the X Games."

"Well, it's because of the image of the company—"

"OK, I won't skate the X Games—but I know I could win at least one contest, maybe not every one, but who knows? If one pays out ten grand and you don't want me to go, then give me ten grand and I won't go."

Bob Burnquist, switch stalefish, backyard, 2002. **Photo:** Grant Brittain

Then they said it was OK to skate the contest. I was getting upset with the way they were controlling what I wanted to do. I had thought I was skateboarding and I didn't have a coach, and all of a sudden I'm back on a team.

I had jumped into the fire. I was now somebody people recognized and connected to a brand, and they wanted to keep that brand association controlled. Deluxe and the crew from San Francisco have a reputation for keeping it the way they want it. I had thought I could change them, but they'd been doing their thing for so long it wasn't like one guy was going to change that. I wanted to be allowed to be in *Transworld*, not just *Thrasher* [*affiliated with Deluxe*]. Why can't I shoot photos with Grant Brittain at *Transworld*? I didn't care about any NorCal versus SoCal—I'm Brazilian. I had moved down to Southern California, and I was living with Jen. Why couldn't I be with the girl I wanted to be with just because she lived in SoCal? There was almost a feeling that when I left San Francisco, I became a traitor.

Mic-E Reyes called and told me I was fired. I started laughing. It was funny being fired as a pro skater when I felt I was still progressing.

I said, "So, that's the exit? Why?"

"I don't know. Go ask Fausto."

I called Fausto, and he told me to go over and hash it out with those guys. I said, "I'm not going to talk to them. I appreciate your help. I'm fired. Thanks for everything."

Julian [*Stranger*] and John [*Cardiel*] were out on a trip, so I couldn't talk to them. It was a weird deal. I still don't know if it was a joke that Mic-E played, or if I was really fired. They called later to try and hash it out, but I was, "No, you fired me. I'm gone."

Even if we could hash it out, it would just come up again.

I talked to Lance [*Mountain*] about the X Games in the mid-'90s. "It's lame because my sponsors don't want me to skate it," I told him. "And at the same time, I've watched the contest on TV, and it sucks."

Lance said, "You can look at it that way and not show up, but the people who do show up will be skateboarding's face."

My whole approach changed after that. The X Games didn't have the right face for the first contest—well, even the second and third ones, all the way down until they hired Chris [*Miller*] and Tony [*Hawk*] and Sal [*Maseakela*] for the commentating. It got more and more legit as it went on.

What you can do is go in and try to create something, and try to change it from the inside, and try to put the right face on it. Today I think it's a legit contest, in the sense that they have good ramps and they have mega and good commentators.

ESPN uses me and I use them. I'm not stoked that they use X Games as a brand to sell boards and bikes. They call it an event, but it's really a brand. In a way, it's like, *Ugh, why do you have to do that?* But then we also get to be on TV and have corporate sponsors involved, so there's a lot more money involved and the skaters can have a livelihood.

I ASSUMED THAT KIDS THOUGHT I SUCKED

<u>Daewon</u> <u>Song</u>: When I was around sixteen, I started going to contests with these guys I'd met at a skate shop, Sporting Ideas. And I finally started watching skate videos. I'd rewind and use that bad VCR pause to try to figure out where the skaters set up their feet. In one video, Mark Gonzales went off a launch ramp switch and did a stalefish. I was like, *What!* That scared me. I couldn't believe it.

I saw *Wheels of Fire* a year after it came out [*1988*], and it made me wish I could be Natas Kaupas. From that point on, I just wanted to progress so fast. I knew some of the spots where Natas skated, like at Paul Revere school, where he did huge frontside wallrides. My friends and I would look at the wall and say, "I bet you this is Natas's mark!"

Pros like Natas and Eric Dressen were like movie stars, and the Bones Brigade were beyond. I got Hosoi's autograph at a contest, and he was one of the coolest dudes ever. He had his spandex shorts on.

Once I got sponsored and started getting free stuff from Rodney, I felt that kids expected a little more from me. It was a little hard to deal with, and I also had the pressure of not wanting to disappoint Rodney. At first I wasn't sure about the whole sponsorship thing. It changed skating from when I was just having fun to people judging me. If I fell or did bad at a contest, I assumed that kids thought I sucked.

They'd see my board all stickered up and ask if I was sponsored. I'd say yes and they'd sort of be like, *Let's see what you got.* Eventually I just got to the point where I skated, and if people thought I sucked, I didn't care.

My first ad was a white-power ad that Steve Rocco did with me, Kareem [*Campbell*], and Daniel [*Castillo*]. Man, Rocco did some funny ads. It was in *Poweredge*, and when a school buddy asked if I still skated, I whipped out the magazine and showed him: "Yeah! Check this out—my first ad! And they say they're going to give me another one!"

But I had no confidence. In '92, when they gave me the "Love Child" song for the video and then named the video *Love Child*, it meant a lot, but it scared me. I had a lot more pros coming up and congratulating me on the part, and companies approached me and wanted to sponsor me. It got to a point where I thought, *Whoa, I'm one of those [pro] guys now.*

It seems like there's more pressure now. Worrying about people judging me shouldn't be in the picture anymore. I'll skate in front of people, and they'll yell, "Do the trick you did in the video! Do your last trick! I know you're skating a mini ramp, but do the switch tre-fakie-manual-fakie-tre-flip."

"There's nowhere to do it."

"Do it on the flat!"

I wonder if when Tony [*Hawk*] does demos they scream for the loop: "Where?"

"Turn the launch ramp! Have somebody flip the ramp while you go around it!"

1   **Tony Hawk**, Andrecht, Carlsbad Pipeline demo, 1983. **Photo:** Grant Brittain
2   **Tony Hawk**, Indy 540, San Diego, 2003. **Photo:** Grant Brittain

I INSTANTLY FEEL THIS PARANOIA

Tony Hawk: Skating has got so big and the stakes are so huge that I rarely go to public skateparks anymore. Part of that is because I have my own ramp, but I don't want to go to a skatepark and try a trick for an hour because people will go home and say I suck. "We saw Tony Hawk at the park and he can't make one trick."

Back then, the only people at a skatepark were the people who loved skating and knew what it took and were there for the hour you tried it, when you made it and when you developed it into something else. Now it's such a public arena and I'm recognizable and when I go to a skatepark, kids sit down and want me to put on a demo. I can't hone my skills, I have to go with demo tricks. If I go to a public skate area, I'm doing a demo whether I like it or not. I'm skating for them when I really just want to skate with them.

I get all introverted. I skate so much with a small group of people on my own ramp that now when I have to do demos, I instantly feel this paranoia. All of a sudden, I'm like *Argh, all these people are watching, here we go, here we go....*I've never felt like that before because I always skated in public. I skated in a skatepark or wherever a contest or demo was and now my regular skating protocol is to skate with my three buddies.

HIGH SCHOOL

Chris Haslam: Daewon wanted me to go pro for Artafakt after Deca ended [*in 2002*], but I said no. I was getting $200 a month on Deca and $500 a month from Artafakt, enough to live on. I just said, "The company is sort of all over the place, and I want to turn pro for something solid." As soon as we got Almost going in 2003, I turned pro. I was twenty-three. I had a couple other sponsors and made maybe two grand a month—livable, but not diamond-necklace money.

Growing up, I was only aware of the skate industry's outside shell. The industry can be a nightmare. Skating is fun, and that's pretty much the only reason I do it. I thought the skateboarding industry was all about how good a skater you can be. That's what I wish it were all about. It was a shock to me that there were these little nonskate things that industry people actually cared about. It's amazing that something small can determine if you make it or break it in skateboarding. It just bums me out that it's gotten to the point where it's not all about the skating anymore.

I don't see how what you look like or what you wear has anything to do with your skating ability. I've actually had people not sponsor me because they were afraid I was going to do a "drastic change" again. "Drastic change"? I went from wearing shitty clothes when I had no money and a shaved head and "changed" into the long hair and beard I have now. [*Laughing*] I was like, *Sweet. This is like high school. I can't get sponsored because I grew my hair out.*

After the Almost video *Round Three* came out, I got known as a pro skater. I was twenty-five and took it as a serious responsibility, but you can still have fun with that responsibility.

IT JUST BUMS ME OUT THAT IT'S GOTTEN TO THE POINT WHERE IT'S NOT ALL ABOUT THE SKATING ANYMORE.

Sometimes I'll find myself falling into the business aspect of skating, and it'll start affecting my skating. That's when I want Singapore status again: phone is off, computer is off, everything is done. I'll go back to Vancouver for a couple of days, skate with my friends, chill out a bit, and then dive back in. Having fun is the main part of my skating, but there is a level to maintain—you have to do your pro deeds, and you need to push yourself and shoot ads and film every once in a while.

WHEN IT ENDS, IT'S DEVASTATING

Dave Hackett: In 1978, I rode for Pepsi, which meant I did demos at anywhere from two or three high schools or junior highs a day all through California, and did demonstrations as part of the "world-famous" Pepsi Skateboard Team. They had a vert ramp with a big Pepsi logo on it. We also did a safety demonstration, and the announcer would explain the importance of wearing the proper equipment.

I did it between contests, because I could make $300 a day doing demos. You could do three a day and you got paid $100 a demo. And we got to man the Pepsi Challenge booth and meet all the hot chicks as they taste-tested colas.

Those Pepsi demos lasted through 1979. I knew the whole industry was coming to an end. There just wasn't a lot of stuff happening. Skating ended abruptly. I was making two to six grand a month—and then nothing. The guy who used to take us to the Pepsi demos was Wink Roberts. He was also our announcer at the Pepsi demos—very animated but very professional. He was always on. Super-nice guy. Wink was an actor and owned the Mr. Roberts painting company. He was the guy who showed me how to paint houses when I was fourteen.

I called him and asked, "Dude, we got any demos coming up?"

"Dude, they cancelled the whole program."

"Really? What am I going to do?"

"Well, we're going to be painting a house in the colony for a movie producer."

"Really? How much can you pay me?"

It was very, very difficult to adjust. As a lifestyle and a living, skateboarding is so bitchin', and when it ends, it's devastating. There's nothing worse than being a has-been or a *was*. And the skateboard industry has such a lack of respect for the guys who built the foundation.

SKATE
SPOTS

THERE ARE SKATEPARKS, BUT THEY ARE COMPARATIVELY FEW AND FAR BETWEEN COMPARED WITH THE LEGALLY SANCTIONED PLAY AREAS THAT OTHER ACTIVITIES ENJOY. And let's be honest—a lot of these skateparks straight-up suck. Take Carlsbad, California, where the city built a horribly designed park next to the police station. The police have strolled over and written tickets for skaters not wearing elbow pads.

And even perfect skateparks aren't sufficient, because the needs of skaters are constantly mutating. "Skate spots" are places where riders skate and hang out. Most are intended for other uses, and the search for handrails or inadvertent banks to walls and double- or triple-sets almost always leads skaters to areas where people don't want them to skate. This trespassing lifestyle shapes the underdog attitude of skaters. Finding your own spots while dodging cops and angry owners demands dedication. Decades ago, artist/writer Craig Stecyk summarized the skater predicament: "Two hundred years of American technology have unwittingly created a massive cement playground of unlimited potential. But it was the minds of eleven-year-olds that could see that potential."

Gonzales pool, 1987. **Photo:** Grant Brittain

IT *LOOKED* LIKE A PROBLEM

<u>Stacy Peralta</u>: We had the drought of 1975 and '76 to support us with pool riding and it made it all possible—you couldn't water your lawn. If your pool was empty, you couldn't fill it up. You were encouraged to flush every fourth time.

We went from skating illegally in public places to private places like backyards. It was the same thing, just different ownership. The first pool we rode was in Bel-Air, on an estate with the pool far removed from the main house. It looked like a big birdbath, so we called it Bird Bath. It was around for about six weeks one summer. The people would hear you, and someone would eventually come out and tell you to leave. You'd play that cat-and-mouse game for a while, and finally the people would either jackhammer the pool or fill it with debris.

The next one was called the Rabbit Hole, a house remodeling in northern Santa Monica where we knew when the construction workers were off, and so we'd ride from four to seven at night. Right after that, there was the Canyon Pool on an abandoned estate. The problem was that Peter Graves, star of the *Mission: Impossible* TV series, lived across the street and hated all this undesirable youth parking their cars, hopping the fence, and spending all day on this estate. He was constantly calling the police. They'd try to scare you. They once actually put us in the back of their car. All of a sudden, sure enough, they had to be somewhere else: "We're letting you guys out, but next time you're in big trouble."

I was around sixteen, and we were terrified. We knew that if we got caught again, we'd be in real trouble because we'd have a mark on us. You did not want that mark. Hal Jepsen and Tony Alva actually did get booked for sneaking into a pool.

We rode the Beverly Hills Keyhole over an entire summer. The Devonshire Pool in the valley—to this day the best backyard pool I've ever ridden—we rode over one summer. Some kid came to the Zephyr shop and told us about it.

Another time I was skateboarding a pool early one morning in the valley. It looked like the house had just been remodeled, a really nice place. I was skating with a couple of my friends who had been invited to skate it with these other two guys, who I didn't know. I finally asked, "How long has this pool been open?"

This guy I didn't know said, "Oh, we drained it last night. The house is for sale. The realtor should be here in a little while."

I went, "Oh, man, I'm out of here! I don't want anything to do with this. They're not going to let you off for this." We took a few more runs and were gone. I never drained a pool. That was serious. That they could pin you for.

[*From '75 to '77*], Escondido Reservoir and the Fruit Bowl always had a massive crowd, because they weren't in people's backyards. The Fruit Bowl was in a condemned sanitarium for fruitcakes so they called it the "Fruit Bowl," and there was nobody around and a lot of space. It could hold a lot of people, and you didn't have to worry about neighbors hearing you. It had a huge, round deep end with a spit gutter on it, which was new, and you could double-carve it. It had a gigantic shallow end. There'd be thirty skaters there sometimes.

Escondido Reservoir was one of the very few hot places to skate in San Diego. That place was so influential and so powerful in its allure that skateparks for years afterward built their own Escondido Reservoirs. I lived in L.A., but whenever I could get down there, I would. It was on the private property of a farm, and any time people would come and see what was going on, they didn't like the element. To an outsider looking in, it looked like a mini Woodstock. There was a rock 'n' roll energy to it. An owner doesn't want that element on his property—a bunch of long-haired people doing something that looks unproductive and makes lots of noise. We looked like bums and vandals to them.

It was heartbreaking when I heard that it had been bulldozed. You get angry, because you know that ultimately you're not hurting anybody. No one was using this thing—it's not even used as a water reservoir anymore. What are we doing wrong? They take it away, and at the same time they condemn kids for doing the wrong things in life. Well, if you'd stop taking away what they're doing that *is* right, maybe they wouldn't do the wrong things.

YOU GET ANGRY, BECAUSE YOU KNOW THAT ULTIMATELY YOU'RE NOT HURTING ANYBODY.

The Fruit Bowl was the same thing. They broke it up as well. Too many people going there, somebody figures out what's going on, and they shut it down. It was a perfectly self-governing situation where fifty to sixty kids went every day and no one got hurt. There was no problem, but it *looked* like a problem. It just had the appearance of a problem, and that appearance was everything they saw—a bunch of grungy kids.

There were a lot of rules at the places we skated. You'd encourage people not to spray-paint, not to leave any evidence you'd been there. It became more acute as we realized we were going to lose this if we didn't take care of it. The first skatepark in California opened up in Carlsbad in 1976, but [*Craig*] Stecyk put it best when he wrote an article asking, "Has any park even matched what currently exists out there that *wasn't* made for skateboarding?" The answer? No.

Around 1976 or '77, we found out about these pipes through kids in Arizona. Warren Bolster got the directions: "Drive to Arizona, and as soon as you pass the border, reset the odometer, because in seventy miles there's going to be a turnoff called Avenue W. There's no gas stations, no stores, nothing—only Avenue W. Loop underneath the highway, make a left, and go straight out to the desert for about twenty minutes. After about five miles, you'll see the tops of pipes on your right. Look for a fence opening."

We had to ditch the Ameron guys, who worked for the company that was putting in this giant water project. We'd skate these pipes and see a truck coming with the guy who'd kick us out. We'd leave for an hour and just come right back.

1

2

1   **Stacy Peralta,** pipes, Arizona, 1977. **Photo:** James Cassimus
2   **Steve Alba,** Black Widow pool, 1988. **Photo:** Grant Brittain

STALEFISH

Skating the pipes was pure magic, the logical extension of pool riding. This was before aerials were invented, so the next obvious thing was to go higher up a vertical wall or past vertical. We also discovered a tunnel of pipes, but after about twelve sections in, it would be pitch-black.

Skating new terrain was totally liberating and mind-expanding, because you'd never done this before, and all of a sudden you're doing it with kind of a relative ease, because we were all ready for the next stage. So when it would happen, we'd jump on it, and the evolution would happen very quickly.

A LOT OF PEOPLE SHARED

Steve Olson: I rode the Fruit Bowl. I rode the Upland L Pool. Baldy. The Egg Bowl. All these pools were in the magazines, and you'd go and ride them. It's the same deal as today, where you go ride a rail that you saw in a magazine.

Skaters in some areas were a little more hush-hush about this shit, about their stuff, but a lot of people shared. I'd give them a pool or a reservoir or a ditch, and they'd give me one.

WE FOUND NINE COW SKULLS, TEN DOG SKULLS

Steve Alba: During the drought that ended in '78, we just barged pools at will. The first time I ever got busted was at 25th and Euclid by this guy called Cyclops. He only had one eye, and his face was scarred up. We had never seen this guy—we'd only heard stories, and while we didn't exactly believe them, I was thirteen and he scared the shit out of me. We heard that he'd take your skateboard away and try to hold you until the cops came.

One day we were skating, and he came charging out of the door running and scared the fuck out of us. We all tried to get over the back wall, but it was tall, and you needed a boost. Three of us got out, but the guy grabbed Mike Martin's leg and pulled him back. Mike was freaking, and the guy was chasing him, and Mike ran the whole way around the pool and came back around, and we pulled him out. Everybody was screaming. We skated it again after that, but we were always on the watch.

When I turned sixteen [in 1976] and got my own car, I really started looking for pools. We'd look for palm trees and those rippled fiberglass fences. We would always drain pools by hand, but we used a pump at the Skull Bowl in the late '70s. It was an old military barracks that had gone to pot, grown over with weeds. The pool was full to the top, and we pumped half of it out and then it got clogged, so we had to drain this black sludge out by hand. It took a month, working three or four days a week—I'm not even shitting you. We found nine cow skulls, ten dog skulls, cat skulls, a bunch of dead birds. That pool stayed open for a good year, until the property sold.

In the late '80s, I'd go flying with a buddy. I'd take photos and then match up the empty pools to a map, marking cross streets. I've ridden at least 1,000 pools. When the earthquake in the valley happened in '94, I skated at least 200 pools in that area alone. There were so many pools in neighborhoods that were red-tagged that you could go down an alleyway and every other house had an empty pool. In the *L.A. Times* they showed a map of devastated areas that were red-tagged. You could skate thirty pools in three blocks. Some pools, you might only take ten runs and never go back. We went out there every weekend for three years, all day long.

It was pool OD, though. It was definitely too much to skate.

AT SKATEPARKS, IT'S *LORD OF THE FLIES*

Lance Mountain: In '76 a magazine said a skatepark was opening in Montebello, which was really close to us. I was blown away when we went there for the first time. It was just three little snake runs with an anthill of people lined up, hundreds of them. We signed up and went to the gate, and they checked our skateboards to see if our trucks were too loose. It was very safety-oriented back then.

I waited in line to ride the snake run, and they told me, "No, you have to go to the beginner area." The beginner area was a sidewalk in a circle. That's what I paid to skate. But those things drive you. There were no skill tests. It was the normal rule of skateboarding: You look at dudes and decide, *That's a new kook.*

Montebello was obsolete by the time it was made, just like most parks at the time. We only skated that park for a year until Lakewood opened.

In a magazine interview, Wally Inouye explained the problem. Most skateparks were being designed by freestylers or slalom racers. They were the more "responsible" skaters that the associations or public could deal with, because they thought that bowl riders were a bunch of losers and punks. Same old thing as today.

The first pool I skated, the Dust Bowl, in '77, was three blocks away from the Montebello skatepark. My friends were pretty good and made friends with Monkey and Louie, the Montebello locals, who showed it to them. I skated it a few times, and I wanted to show it to my parents.

They drove me over and pulled into the driveway. I ran in ahead, and by the time they got around the back, I was lying on the bottom of the pool knocked out. I don't know what I did. I don't even know the story. I only know what my sister told me. I was in the hospital and unconscious and incoherent for five hours.

My parents took my skateboard away. "You're not doing that anymore." Then it was, "You have to wear a helmet." I had one of those little yellow Cooper [*hockey*] helmets.

Monkey and Louie told me that I couldn't ride their new pool. They'd let me go but made me wear my helmet just to watch. It was full skateboard teasing, vibing. They were the guys that made me think, *I have to prove myself to these guys.*

The first time I ever saw vert skating properly was in '77 at the Baker Pool—a guy hitting the lip, one-wheeling, one-wheeling, one-wheeling, pumping wheelers, putting his hand behind his back. We thought, *Oh, that's how you skateboard.*

I didn't skate that day. I just sat on the stairs and watched. If you showed up to a session with ripping dudes, you didn't skate. Now you do, but then you didn't. It was the first time we saw live vertical pool skating done right. Before that, we were

Tony Hawk, crossbone air, Del Mar, 1987. **Photo:** Grant Brittain

trying to figure it out from the magazines. Then it was on. We were trying to find every pool we could skate.

Whittier Skate City opened up at the end of '79, when I was sixteen, and that's when I really became a skatepark kid. Normally, at Lakewood, ten or fifteen people skated, and then one weekend nobody was there. One guy finally showed up, and I asked why it was so empty. "Whittier Skate City opened," he said. One weekend Lakewood was pretty crowded, and the next it was dead.

I wasn't bummed—I just asked where Whittier was. The first time I skated it, they asked me to be on the park team. The thing about Whittier was that everybody there was rich. They rode brand-new Caster boards, brand-new gyros, and then the next week, whatever was hot, they had. I rode junk and looked like a total bum. I'd show up with homemade boards, but I think that earned me some respect.

Being on the Skate City team meant free equipment, but the skate shop only had six boards in it for the whole two years it was open. Ray Bones and Daryl Miller and George Orton were locals there, and they started giving me stuff.

It took around two hours to bus to Whittier. I skated there once, and that took eight hours. At that time, skateboarding was an adventure, just finding spots and going to new places. I'd take the bus through Watts to Marina skatepark. One time on the bus, there was a full knife fight. It didn't stop us from taking the bus to Marina—we just didn't tell our parents.

I started working at Whittier when skateboarding was really unpopular, in '82. There was hardly anyone there except for [John] Lucero, [Neil] Blender, [Lester] Kasai, and a bunch of local guys.

Sometimes we slept over in the parking lot. We had a band because we could, and we played in a loft above the park. There were no parents at skateparks any-more, and we were sixteen and seventeen, and we could go anywhere, do anything, just wake up and skate and mess around.

Whittier probably never made money. They had me come in at noon to open the arcade because two people wanted to use some quarters. They'd pay me $3.75 an hour to make fifty cents. The owner was never there, but his two sons were, and they joined in until things got out of hand. "Out of hand" would be like the time the skatepark put highball trampolines in so all the jocks would come and play in them. One skater put bricks in the highball, and when the guys came in and jumped, a brick hit one of the dudes. When you injured somebody outside of skateboarding, it was going too far. There was a kid, Mark Poots, who was duct-taped up, put in a trash can, dropped into the pool, and left there, and that was fine.

I was so lame. The locals owned Whittier—we knew every inch of it. When other people were skating, we'd drop in on them: "Coming in!" There was a new fourteen-year-old, called Bubbles because he was a little chunky. He was learning how to skate. Lucero or somebody said, "Let's roll in on him every time he rolls in." We did it over and over, until he was almost in tears, and then I finally ran him over and broke his toe. At skateparks, it's Lord of the Flies. If one kid can't cope, then he gets tortured. People did it to me, and I could take it, so I never thought it was lame.

There was a kid, Mark Poots, who was duct-taped up, put in a trash can, dropped into the pool, and left there, and that was fine. —Lance Mountain

The owner just sold the land in '83. Most skateparks closed around that time, 'cause the land was worth more than the proceeds from five people skating for five dollars a day. Dentists and doctors owned a lot of the 1970s skateparks. From what I understand, it was written up in investment journals that skateparks were a good investment.

A LOT OF THE BADLANDS LOCALS WOULD THROW ROCKS AT YOUR CARS

Steve Alba: The Dogtown thing is overblown, in that they claim they made up pool riding in the '70s, but we can actually say that in the Badlands, we made up pipe riding. Pat Mullus found Baldy. Supposedly they used to trip out on acid in the '60s and walk into this spillway to spray-paint or throw rocks or whatever. One day they walked the other way and ran into the pipe. They were tripping out on how it echoes in there—it makes all these weird noises once you're in the pipe.

Around '76, or maybe earlier, we skated Baldy for the first time. When we skated L Pool, some of the older Badlands skaters were talking about it, and a week later we went there. We walked around for six hours until we found it. We were completely clueless thirteen-year-old kids.

If you parked on top of the hill, cops could see your car and know you were there. A lot of the Badlands locals would throw rocks at your cars, smash your windshield, flatten your tires, to keep nonlocals away. From '75 to '78, there were twenty or more people there every day. I saw most of the good guys ride there, like Waldo [Autry], [Rick] Blackheart, Greg Ayres, Stacy Peralta. Then, in the summer of '78, they tarred the whole pipe to keep us out, and that was fucked.

It was out of commission for a couple of years. We took spackling knives and chipped off the tar. It took forever, but we'd just clear an area and skate. It wasn't until '84 that the Tar Era ended.

MY FIRST KISS WAS BEHIND THE WINDMILL

Tony Hawk: Del Mar skatepark was where all my friends were and my home away from home. There were four school buses that had different routes, and I figured out what bus dropped off closest to the skatepark. Every day after school, I'd catch the bus and skate until my dad picked me up, usually at eight or nine. Del Mar was it—that's really the only place I went. I didn't go to any school functions, no football games, dances, or parties—none of it. The only thing I showed up for was when I got my diploma, and then I was out.

It was my place of recreation, it's where all my friends were, it's where I met girls. Del Mar also had highball, miniature golf, a driving range, and an off-road RC track. My first kiss was behind the windmill on the miniature-golf course.

My big weakness was that I couldn't skate well in other places—only Del Mar. Every park had a different transition, size of bowl, amount of vert. Del Mar had way more flat bottom than any other place, and only two walls that were really good on it. It might have been eight-and-a-half-foot transitions with a foot of vert. Upland was twelve feet deep and super-steep, and the coping was giant. If you fell, it was so rough that your kneepads were pulled off. It felt like death. I eventually learned to adapt.

FLAMES WERE SHOOTING OUT FROM UNDERNEATH THE RAMP

<u>Kevin Harris</u>: The first ramp I built in my backyard was in 1976. We knew we had to copy a pool transition, but we had no idea how to do that. We nailed two-by-fours into giant crosses and tried to line them up to make a transition. My skate friend Mark Richtor laughed at us: "You guys are doing this all wrong! I built my own ramp—this is what you have to do." Richtor's ramp leaned against a thick, thorny patch of bushes, and he'd nailed in a few support beams.

BUT THE FIRST FEW RAMPS WERE AWFUL. IF WE HAD TOO MANY PEOPLE ON THE DECK, THE RAMP WOULD SWAY.

At that time, my house was surrounded by farmland that was being subdivided, and homes were going up like crazy. These construction sites had piles of wood, and at night a few of us would walk up and grab some. As we carried it home, we'd see headlights, everybody would yell, "Car!" and we'd dump the wood and run.

My mom would be washing the supper dishes, watching all of us drag wood into her backyard. She'd just wave at us. For some reason, I never considered it stealing, even though we probably took hundreds of sheets of plywood and even more two-by-fours. It was like skating somebody's backyard pool—I never thought, *OK, I'm skating something that belongs to somebody else. I'm trespassing.* One time when I was in fifth grade, I took a bag of chips from school and felt so bad that I went back the next day and paid for it. I've never stolen anything in my life since. We weren't stealing for profit, and there were no skateparks or anything to skate. In my mind, at that time, it was what we had to do to skate.

Seeing new ramps in *SkateBoarder* magazine dictated when to rebuild, and most ramps didn't last more than a year. More experienced skaters would show up to skate and give us tips on how to cut out transitions. But the first few ramps were awful. If we had too many people on the deck, the ramp would sway. There were always six core guys who helped build the ramp and then, without fail, seriously, on the day it was finished skaters would pour in. It was as if that last nail sent them a message. Gnarly, drug-addicted East Vancouver skaters would walk into my back-yard, and then some nervous Beaver Cleaver kid in a rickety hockey helmet with a banana board would walk in.

In '78 or '79, we built the state-of-the-art ramp for the time: Sixteen feet wide with ten-foot trannies and a foot of vert. We even stained the wood grass green and had pool coping. The traffic suddenly got a lot more upscale, with visitors from California. Tony Alva, Shogo Kubo, Frank Blood—these were legends, and they'd just walk into my backyard. My mom would cook up these huge pots of chili for everybody. At night, I'd lie in bed thinking, *Oh, my God! Shogo Kubo skated my backyard! He knows my name! And he likes my ramp!*

We had a neighbor who hated us and would scream at us with his heavy eastern European accent. In November of '79, the air was foggy, and frost coated the ground. I was coming back with my parents from dinner, and we saw a glow from our backyard. We ran around the back, and flames were shooting out from underneath the ramp. We hosed it down, threw buckets of water on it. Once the fire was out, we noticed that the frosted grass showed a trail of footprints that trekked across our lawn and back into our crazed neighbor's house. We called the cops, and they went and talked to him and left without even talking to us again. They didn't treat it like arson or anything. The ramp was charred, but the structure was still sound.

I got married and moved out in 1982. In 1984, my parents sold the house and asked me to tear down the ramp. I couldn't do it. I was a total wreck during the weekend the ramp was being torn down. It held more memories than the house I grew up in. I would not have been able to cut into it. I feel like crap that my dad had to tear it down single-handedly, but I wouldn't even be able to do it now, twenty-two years later. To this day, I've never seen my old yard after the ramp was gone.

ALL THESE KIDS FLYING DOWN THE HILL PROBABLY LOOKED PRETTY FRIGHTENING

Tommy Guerrero: In the early '80s, I remember skating Milpitas skatepark and other parks and how it was so fun and awesome. They let us down, basically, when they closed. I cut up all my skatepark cards. They pissed us off. I don't remember exactly what the emotion was, but I do remember anger, lashing out: "Fuck that shit—stupid skateparks." If I wanted to skate, I'd go skate down the block. And everybody was playing backyard bandit, searching out pools again, finding skate spots, the banks, the ditches—really searching for terrain again.

I'd been skating the hills since I was ten. People would spray water at you from their driveways, or spray their driveways down so you couldn't skate them. That was the first antiskate device: water. There was a woman who threw buckets of water out her window, and I got hit once. She could tell when we were coming—it's so loud when a bunch of kids come down the hill—and something came out the window and got me.

The 9th Avenue run was a series of hills, and we'd take the bus up and skate down. Sometimes twenty-plus kids would be flying down the hills. Cars didn't watch out for you—no one cared, and that didn't even come into play. There was one street that was really busy, and people would just be like, *What the fuck?* All these kids flying down the hill probably looked pretty frightening.

THAT SAVED ME. SAVED EVERYBODY.

Jamie Thomas: I'll drive by interesting architecture that I can skate or find out about a spot from a video. It feels best to find skate spots yourself, though—it's more real. If it's some office with people coming in and out, you know you won't be able to skate there in the daytime. It's common sense to know when you can skate it without being busted. It's not the same as trying to figure out when to skate a backyard pool—a lot of street spots post the hours you can skate right on the front window. The sign basically says, "Be here when it's *not* these hours. Wait an hour after closing, and it's fine."

That doesn't always work. I spent the night in jail for skating a rail. I was skating with Erik Ellington, and he'd almost made this boardslide on a curved rail when the security guard kicked us out. We came back later, and he called the cops. The owner of the complex pressed trespassing charges, and it's on my record. Every time I go through customs, they ask me what I was arrested for.

I tried to skate this double kink in Arizona on a tour and got kicked out. I thought I'd just come back on another tour and skate it again, but as time went on, the video deadline grew closer, and I wanted it in my part. So I drove out to Phoenix with Atiba Jefferson and Lee Dupont to try and get it. We left San Diego at about half past six in the evening and got there at one in the morning. We skated for almost an hour, and just as I was riding away from the trick, the security guard came around and kicked us out. We just packed it up and got home at six.

That was fun. Some people might not think that's fun, but that was a big challenge to me. It was a big roll of the dice, because all three of us knew that when we left, we would return either really, really psyched or really, really bummed.

I've set up situations like that before and not made it. I have taken the drive of shame all the way home afterward. I'll be thinking about how I have to stop putting myself in scenarios like this. I've gotten to skate spots and started seeing double vision because I put so much pressure on myself that I can't focus, no matter how hard I try. I used to just go for it anyway, and I actually got knocked out and jacked up a few times skating under those conditions.

In 1996, I went to Point Loma High School with a random crew of skaters and a photographer to check out a twelve-stair handrail. We were all skating this one spot, and I realized I'd forgotten something in my car. On the way back, I rolled up to this rail and I thought, *Holy crap! That's a big drop! That's probably a vert ramp plus five, six feet.* I had always tried to calculate the biggest drop I could physically withstand, and I wanted to test it at some point.

I thought this gap was possible, maybe around eighteen feet down, around two stories into this pit. There was nobody with me, so I wasn't going to try it, in case I broke myself and got stuck in the pit. The only way out was up the stairs. I decided to push up to it at full speed, just to get a feeling of what it'd be like to really try it. I pushed toward it and kicked my board up at the last moment and grabbed the handrail to stop myself. I looked down and saw "Jamie M Thomas Gap" written in white pen on the rail. It was right where I'd grabbed it.

I got the shivers and got kind of freaked out. I was by myself and really in a weird place. I got the other skaters and showed them the gap, and they said, "Nobody can do that!"

"I think I can," I said. "And look at this!" I showed them the rail, and they kind of freaked out.

"Did you write that?"

"*No!* Why would I write that? It was already there."

For the next six months, I'd go look at the gap and think about doing it, and eventually I said I wanted to do it.

I remember dropping in the air and thinking, *Dude, this is way higher than I imagined.*

–Jamie Thomas

It's the scariest thing that I've done to this day. I put my board down and climbed over the rail and jumped down to see if the impact wasn't too ridiculous. I rolled out of it OK, so that was good, but just jumping off it freaked the other skaters and Grant [*Brittain*] out.

In the early Zero days, my friends and I had this commitment handshake, and it meant "land—or slam." It was a promise based on what Zero was all about, and the trust between us meant I'd try to land it. I called Adrian [*Lopez*] up, met him in the middle of the stairs, and we shook.

I went back to the starting point, bent down to tie my shoe, and looked to my right and saw a dead bird. *Oh, no,* I thought. *I hope that's not an omen. Oh, well, I gave the handshake.*…I pushed toward it and was completely, absolutely frightened, but I was trying to breathe through it. I've faced things before when you're pushing up to things and you don't really know if it's going to be good for you. I pushed off and ollied over it.

I remember dropping in the air and thinking, *Dude, this is* way *higher than I imagined. There's no way I'm going to be riding away from this. No way.*

Then: *I just did something wrong. What did I get myself into?*

It was a *lot* different than just jumping off the rail. I landed, and my board broke and I rolled out of it. My ankle was hurting. My hip hit the ground kind of hard. It took a lot out of me, and there was no way I'd have been able to set up another board to try it again. But I felt really, really lucky to be walking away from it.

We were putting together my first Zero ad and using that gap ollie as the image. I asked Adrian if he had a name for the gap. He just blurted out, "Leap of Faith." I was surprised at the response from the skateboarders. Danny Way came up and told me it was nuts. I was flattered: *Whoa, Danny Way thinks that's nuts.*…

"But I didn't even make it," I said.

"That doesn't matter," he said. "Just trying that is gnarly."

I was already on to other things after my ankle healed two weeks later. I wanted to try it again, but I was never injury-free, and that's not something you want to try with an injury. Now there's an elevator built into the area where I ollied. That saved me. Saved everybody.

I'D CRY OUT OF FRUSTRATION MORE THAN OUT OF PAIN

Bob Burnquist: Skateboarding can teach you self-esteem and other things, but it can throw a bit of a selfish air into you if you don't interact as a group. At a skatepark, your skating is all about you, but what's the fun in doing it alone? It's about you and at least one other friend you can share it with.

When I was eleven, I started skating the Ultra Skatepark. It was built on the property of the Ultra Tile business. It was the best park around, and people from all different parts of Brazil came. It became a hub. We were the Ultra Boys. But it took me a while to get my foot in the Ultra door. I had to make friends on my own, instead of being on a team or having my parents involved.

The first time I dropped in, I went straight to my face. Dropping in on vert looked so easy. I couldn't even drop in on a mini ramp. I put my pads on and walked up to the vert ramp deck. I put my board down, and the other skaters asked me if I'd ever dropped in before.

"No, it's my first time."

They gave me some pointers. I did the sign of the cross on my chest and then just stepped on my board. I thought you just had to go. I went over and straight to my face, straight down. My face had blood on it. I was so pissed. Everybody was tripping, trying to see if I was OK. I grabbed my board and went up the stairs again and put my board down to drop in again. The skaters were telling me not to do it again. But I went, then *Boom!* I slammed the same exact way. After that slam, people were laughing and saying, "You can't even drop in on the mini ramp."

"Yes, I can!" I screamed at them.

"You can't even drop in on *this* ramp!" It was a tiny four-footer.

"Yes, I can!"

"OK, then do it."

I dropped in a third time and slammed. *Everybody* was laughing. I grabbed my board and left. I was so pissed off. All I learned was that all those guys were laughing at me and I wanted to prove something to them. It was pure emotion, no thinking.

When I was around thirteen, all my friends were older skaters by at least two years, and I wanted their skills immediately. I became known as the guy who slammed, and people would tell me to calm down. I'd do frontside rocks and hit my trucks on the way in and *boom* to the flat bottom on my chest. I'd hardly be able to breathe and be crying on the ramp. I'd cry out of frustration more than out of pain.

Skaters torture each other at skateparks. If you've got skills, then people respect you—it's not about money. That's what I like about skateparks—it's all about your abilities. There could be the richest kid with the best gear, and then there could be the most ragged kid with the worst gear but he kills and he's got style, and in there he has the respect. But it's also not the rich kid's fault—he just has money and he's stoked on skating. There was one kid like that at our park, but he was cool. He wouldn't flash on us and he'd let us ride his board, and he'd hook us up with stickers.

A BACK-ALLEY KIND OF PLACE

Kevin Harris: After I started skating in '75, I would meet with the city council to try and get a public skatepark in my town. One council member actually told me that when I was nineteen I'd get a girlfriend and stop skating and caring if there was a skatepark.

By the mid-'80s, when I could financially afford to do it on my own, I said, "Screw the city. I'll do this on my own." I put ten grand in, and we rented a ware-house in an industrial part of town. Nobody with a nice warehouse would rent to skaters. It took two weeks to set up the vert ramp from Expo '86 and some ramps and we called it the Richmond Skate Ranch. It was sketchy. The seven-foot ramp got a hole in it the first day. No joke—we had to fix that thing every three days.

Eventually we got Lance [*Mountain*] to build us ramps, and they were awesome. But the Ranch was only awesome to skaters. It wasn't all clean, like a Vans skatepark is nowadays. It smelled like sour pads and sweat, and Masonite dust caked up in your nose. But we weren't trying to impress anybody but skateboarders. If parents had been hanging out like they do at baseball games, then we would have made it more parent-friendly. Parents only stepped into the place to sign the waiver form. Most of them didn't even look into the place and see what was there.

Colin McKay once described the Ranch as a back-alley kind of place, and I think he meant that as a compliment. Even if we had leather couches and a cappuccino machine, the parents wouldn't have hung out—they didn't exist. Now you have parents at skateparks coaching—completely different atmosphere from the mid-'80s.

I had to close the Ranch in 1993, and I was seriously depressed. But since then, I've had sixty to eighty random people introduce themselves and start talking about it. Some guys—guys with tattoos, rough characters—teared up, saying it was the best time of their lives. They'll shake my hand, look me in the eyes, and say, "No, really. I mean it. Thank you."

There were guys who lived at the Ranch. I knew when I showed up at seven at night that the regular guys were going to be there. Even if they weren't skating, they'd just be hanging out. Some people grew up at the park in a sense. There was an amazing sense of brotherhood. It could get crazy in there, and there were sleepovers and complaints from the women's-workout place next door, and the locals would travel in a pack, and I'd hear all these bus-ride-home nightmare stories. There was always some bet that involved getting a skater to drink some disgusting mixture of pad-sweat drippings and mustard and coffee grinds and Sprite for four bucks. We had bands come in and all-night skate sessions. Some employees got all into Ouija boards, and some people thought the place was haunted.

I was taken aback by the emotion of the skaters thanking me, because the Ranch ended sort of crappy. Some skaters thought I made money off of them because they had to pay to skate. I had a successful skateboard-distribution company that supported the Ranch. By the end, I had lost $50,000 on it, but skaters were punching holes in the walls, spray-painting around the building. Nobody ever thanked me while the park was going. But even I didn't fully understand the value of the Ranch until it was gone.

It'd be really, really hard to duplicate that feeling at a park again. I tried to with Colin when we did RDS Skatepark, and it didn't work. It's a different era of skating nowadays. Skating is in a different place and really popular and accepted. That sense of community on a small scale is gone.

IN THE JAPANESE LANGUAGE, *UCHI-SOTO* DEFINES THE DISTINCTION BETWEEN IN-GROUPS AND OUT-GROUPS. Participating in an activity that is outlawed in most areas is a good way to experience that distinction. That's why skateboarding has historically attracted the disenfranchised and produces a subculture so tight that it can retard social growth. And most skaters are fine, if not downright happy, about this. When you become accustomed to hassles from nonskaters, to running from security guards and cops, and you refer to one another as dirtbags, rejects, skate rats, mass acceptance can make you feel like you switched from the in-group to the out-group.

Steve Alba, Mount Baldy, 2001. **Photo:** Grant Brittain

1

2

3

1   **Steve Olson** and **Duane Peters,** 2005. **Photo:** Grant Brittain
2   **Lance Mountain,** Trashmore, 1985. **Photo:** Grant Brittain
3   **Mike Vallely,** Powell ad, 1988. **Photo:** Courtesy of George Powell

STALEFISH

WAIT A SECOND...THIS ISN'T WHAT WE WANT

<u>Stacy</u> <u>Peralta</u>: I changed. I actually wanted to see skateboarding as a sport in the 1970s. Such a big part of my life was introducing skateboarding to the world. We were the first wave of skateboarders that traveled around the world to introduce skateboarding to places and people that had never seen it. I fell into that, and I got into the spiel of constantly explaining it to journalists. I believed at that time that "yes, it is a sport, and it is going to go to the Olympics."

It wasn't until I started Powell Peralta that I thought, *Wait a second…this isn't what we want. We want to hold contests in backyards; we don't want to have anything to do with the Olympic Committee.*

I realized that's really what skateboarding was about and what was really fun for me as a kid—hopping over fences and riding in pools and other places, and the liberation of not having adults around. It was just a realization of what skateboarding really is. It really is a liberal activity.

The Little League commentary during the parking-lot contest in *Future Primitive* was our way of saying where we didn't want skateboarding to go. Here's this contest that's going beautifully well. It's total chaos, there's the denting of a car in the middle—it's beautiful. And so what we really need right now is to have somebody come in and say, "Let's package this. Let's get these guys in uniforms. Let's make a lot of money off it." That was our way of poking fun at that ideal. No, the way it is is perfect. We had experienced the beginnings of that ideal, and that's not where skateboarding wanted to go, which is ultimately to the Olympics, where it doesn't belong.

The Olympic Committee paid skateboarding the greatest compliment by choosing snowboarding—which is a younger sport and an offshoot of skateboarding—over skateboarding. They don't know how to corral skateboarders—it doesn't fit their image.

SKATEBOARDING AND PUNK ROCK WERE A SMALL MARRIAGE THAT WAS MEANT TO BE

<u>Steve</u> <u>Olson</u>: At the first Hester series at Spring Valley, in '78, I heard Mink DeVille and the Ramones, and it was like, "Wow, that's pretty dope music." It had some '50s, a little bit of surf—it was cool.

At Newark it exploded. I was working on the trucks with those dudes at Santa Cruz, so I was always up at the city [*San Francisco*] as well. Then one dude showed up at the contest, this cat Terry Nails, he downhilled, and he was dressed really cool-looking. He was total punk rocker. And then it was totally over for me.

I just dug the music and dug that I could dress this weird way. It wasn't accepted. Skating was somewhat accepted, but you were looked down upon, as if you were riding a toy. I never went around saying I was a world-champion skateboarder. People would have just said, "Oh, really? That's great. So what? You're a world-champion toy rider. Aren't you too old?"

"I'm sixteen!"

"Yeah, but isn't that thing designed for seven-year-olds?"

At the time, it was not cool in the punk world to be a skateboarder. You were looked down on there, too. That had changed by the early '80s. Skating and punk went hand in hand. The original punk people were older art people, and then the beach kids came in and it went to where it went. Punk was already over in England and New York, but it was going strong in L.A. and San Francisco. It was excellent. It had the whole "fuck you" attitude.

One of the big turning points took place at a contest at Winchester, in San Jose, in '79. When some of us didn't make the cut to the finals, we went up to a gig in San Francisco with the Clash, the Cramps, and the Dead Kennedys. It was me, Alva, and Salba. We had started dressing like punk rockers, and that was when it really hit huge. We were out there pogoing around, throwing each other around. It was totally fun and spastic and careless. It was just like throwing yourself into the pool and slamming. It was the best time. Skateboarding and punk rock were a small marriage that was meant to be.

BUT I WASN'T GOING TO SAY IT, SO THEY PUNCHED ME

<u>Lance</u> <u>Mountain</u>: The first time I heard punk was at a Lakewood pro contest in '79. Doug Saladino skated to Blondie. Salba wore a Devo shirt. Instantly I went out and got that music. Alva and those guys had been ratty little surf kids with their cool Dogtown hand-drawn boards, and then, *boom!*, in '79 products are Day-Glo and there's new music. You didn't hear Ted Nugent anymore.

Punk started as quirky weirdos, artistic dudes. Devo and 999 and that kind of rad punk is almost retarded, and the people who liked it were retarded kind of people, like skaters. For me, it was really close to skateboarding without using a skateboard.

We knew skateboarding was really special, but we were the only five people in the world who knew that. Skaters say, "In the '80s, if you skateboarded, you were hated." You weren't hated. You weren't noticed. You knew what you were doing was special, and so the best way to let them know, to get noticed, was to piss them off. It's almost fun to make them think, *What is wrong with you?*

Punk was the same attitude of *We're going to show you so you have to take notice.*

In high school, during gym class, a few guys held me down: "Tell us punk sucks." It was the stupidest thing on Earth. I thought, *It's so rad that you guys are so annoyed.* But I wasn't going to say it, so they punched me.

In '77 and '78, skateboarding was almost cool, but as it started dying and you got older, it was totally dumb, and punk came into skating. In the '80s, things got rowdier and crazier, and it was harder for me to fit in. I went to church on my own, and I'd get these stares and attitude like, *What's this sinner doing? He's doing an evil activity.* So I pretty much didn't fit in there. And then all my skater friends knew I was a Christian, so I was a goody-goody retard to them. I always felt that the whole skating thing is a reach to get your peers' respect, for them to think you're good. So I was always under that, and I didn't really have high self-esteem. I think a lot of skaters lack self-esteem, even within skating, and that's what drives them.

SKATEBOARDER! SKATEBOARDER! SING!

<u>Mike</u> <u>Vallely</u>: I went in for a routine physical when I was fifteen, in '85. The doctor took one look at my legs and said, "Oh, my God!" There was so much damage to my shins and hips and knees—I skated more and took more falls than anybody. I was almost masochistic in my approach to skating.

The doctor's tone got very serious. I didn't understand what he was talking about, and he straight out asked me, "Who's hurting you?"

"What do you mean?"

"Your legs!"

"Oh, that's from skateboarding."

Then he got mad at me. "How can you do this to yourself? Why would you do something that's so destructive to your body?"

"Because it's fun."

"That's fun?"

"Yeah, it's fun."

He told my parents that I wouldn't be able to walk in ten years. They were just like, "Don't even go there. We can't stop him."

Very early on, a skater decides to continue or to stop. The first bad slam or tooth knocked out or bone popped through the skin—you either go, *Aw, man, this isn't for me*, or you accept it as part of the equation.

THEN HE GOT MAD AT ME. "HOW CAN YOU DO THIS TO YOURSELF? WHY WOULD YOU DO SOMETHING THAT'S SO DESTRUCTIVE TO YOUR BODY?"

The next year, in '86, some casting agent called my house about auditioning in New York for a McDonald's commercial that paid $10,000. I went into a room with fifteen kids. One spun a basketball, one was a cheerleader, one had a baton, and they were all standing in a big semicircle in front of a camera. Someone told me to get in there and then they started playing, very loud, a McDonald's jingle over a PA system. They wanted everybody to sing along and show off their talent. The cheerleader starts jumping in the air, the basketball kid is spinning and singing his jingle, and I'm standing there holding my skateboard.

The director starts yelling at me, "Skateboarder! Skateboarder! Sing!"

"No, I don't sing."

"Do some tricks!"

"What? It's all carpeted!"

All the kids were encouraging me and started yelling, "Come on, skateboarder! Come on!"

I did a ho-ho plant, and everybody started clapping. The director yells, "That's great! Great!"

As soon as I landed it, I picked up my skateboard and walked out of the room. Tears were burning down my cheek. I felt ill. *This isn't what I care about. This isn't why I started skateboarding.*

I walked past my dad and went and hid for twenty minutes. I needed time to figure it out. It felt silly, and with that McDonald's jingle playing…it wasn't skateboarding.

I didn't get the commercial.

A STEP ABOVE GANGBANGING

Daewon Song: If I'm on long flights, I'll be flipping through a skate mag and somebody notices and starts talking. Then the question comes up: "What do you do for a living?"

When I say that I skateboard, they don't always understand. "What, do you have a show?" I'm not defensive, because it's not their fault. I just tell them it's a weird thing how professional skateboarding works. I explain how it's an individual sport where you're in charge of your progression and what you're doing.

"You kind of make your money though endorsements and sponsors, or you can tie yourself in with the companies."

They get pretty excited, because they knew nothing about it. They can see skaters and know what they're up to, instead of thinking that they're just troublemakers.

Skateboarding used to be thought of as a step above gangbanging, at one point. A parent did not want you to skateboard. I want people to understand skateboarding.

IF YOU WERE WEARING VANS IN '86, YOU WERE A SKATER

Tony Hawk: When skating became somewhat more popular, around 1985, you found a sense of community, and people really embraced the music and the fashion—the culture of skating. It was underground, but it was edgy and really cool. It wasn't like today, where regular people look like skaters—you could tell a skater by sight. They might have had long bangs or have been wearing dirty jeans and Vans. This was before Vans retail outlets—if you were wearing Vans in '86, you were a skater.

In the '80s, going to a skate shop was your salvation. That's where they spoke your language and where you felt you belonged. A skate shop was the only way to disperse the information and the passion. A lot of time they weren't even purely skate shops, they were head shops that maybe sold decks.

It was strange for me that the same people who had discounted skating in the '80s and '90s were inviting guys like me to A-list events ten years later. For a while, I drank the Kool-Aid. I thought you had to buy suits and look like somebody you see on the red carpet, or they wouldn't let you in the event. But after the novelty wore off, I realized, *I don't care what they think of me. I'm going to dress like I normally do, and if that's not good enough for them, then whatever.*

Tony Hawk, Sanoland, 1983. Photo: Grant Brittain

YOU'RE GOING TO STOP SKATING AND GROW A MUSTACHE

<u>Lance Mountain</u>: Skateboarding was a trendy thing to do, and there were a lot of freestyle girls when I started in the mid-'70s. But the girls died off when vert caught on.

My skater friends didn't have steady girlfriends. They just slept with groupie girls. There were definitely no popular girls around skateboarders. It was all the girls that had some sort of problems. I didn't sleep around, and I thought I wasn't abusing these girls, but I guess I was when I lit their hair on fire and things like that.

I met Yvette when I was sixteen. It was weird for me, because I didn't think I'd ever have a girlfriend. I wasn't interested—I was a skateboarder. Either you skated, or you tried to be cool and get a girlfriend. Yvette was more like a best friend for the first two years. She's a really good viber, and none of my friends liked her. She wasn't there to kiss anybody's butt. It did get weird when we all went to Europe in 1983, and my friends told me to choose them or her. I was like, "OK, bye!" to them. But I understood—you can't throw a girl in there, because you're betraying the pirates.

In the early '80s, all the older pros got girlfriends and smoked cigarettes and then left skateboarding. So if you got a girlfriend, it was like "growing up" to be like them. They seemed ten or fifteen years older than us, when really they were only two years older at the most. So the equation was: Get a car and a girlfriend and that makes you old, and you're going to stop skating and grow a mustache. That says more than anything about how skateboarding can stunt your growth.

I got married at twenty, and then I had a kid. Skaters didn't do that. I felt like an idiot with a kid. I felt totally immature. I was the only one in my peer group who was married. Part of me didn't want to get married, because that meant I'd have to grow up. I know there was a scare from Powell: *Should we let people know that Lance is married? Is it bad for sales?* Once they thought my son could help sell mini boards, once it was decided to be good for business, then he was in an ad.

But I don't blame anybody. I remember thinking as a kid that any skater with a mustache was an old man. Mustache equaled old man, and old is bad in skating.

THAT'S THE TEST OF WHETHER YOU CAN SURVIVE IN THE SKATE GAME

<u>Daewon Song</u>: I didn't do any of the school functions. I had a few crushes, but whatever—skating always came first. I had a girlfriend in junior high, and she'd say, "You want to go get a burger?"

I'd say, "Ahhh, I'm going to meet people to go skate this jump ramp."

After a while, I was over it. I didn't get a real girlfriend until I was eighteen, nineteen. I get scared for the new generation. They're fifteen or sixteen right now, then they'll get a girl, and that's the test of whether you can survive in the skate game. When you get that first taste…whoa, that can change a lot of things. I didn't get involved with girls, you know, on that level, until I was nineteen. Isn't that crazy? Some girls get controlling, and I didn't want that.

I COULDN'T BELIEVE THAT I HAD ALMOST LOST THE BEST THING IN MY LIFE. IT SCARED ME. IT MADE ME REALIZE HOW STUPID I WAS. I ALMOST RUINED MY LIFE.

But in 1993, I got hooked on my first serious girlfriend, and I started veering away from skating. And I started dropping cars. Skateboarding had taken a plunge, and I thought, *I love dropping cars! I could drop cars for a living!* And I bought a Makita cutter. I had broken my ankle and wasn't skating as much anymore. It took me a while to get better, and I had a whole new lifestyle. I wasn't even around other skaters, just with this girl. World Industries considered kicking me off, and I didn't really care. I just got lazy. I was looking for something else. The girl thing really messed it up. I was with her for seven years.

Then a lot of the riders left the company and started Girl skateboards, and Rodney was seriously bummed out. It almost killed the company, and seeing Rodney go through that pain made me realize I had to support him. He had always supported me. That's when I woke up. I said, "Rodney, I promise you that I'm going to skate more, and we're going to get through this. I guess it's just me and you." We started doing all these videos and tried to go full-force.

I couldn't believe that I had almost lost the best thing in my life. It scared me. It made me realize how stupid I was. I almost ruined my life.

IT WAS ALWAYS FOR PEOPLE WHO GOT SHUNNED BY THE MASSES

Tommy Guerrero: Skating is almost respected to some degree, and you're like, *Man, that sucks! What is that? They don't know.*

And then some people say skating is a sport. Sport? I'm not wearing a number. I'm not on a fucking team. This isn't a team thing here. I'm not going out with ten guys trying to do a backside air.

Give me a fucking break. I don't agree that it is a sport and I never did, because it was always for people who got shunned by the masses, and sports are not like that at all.

WEAPONS
OF MASS
PROPAGANDA

SKATERS HAVE ALWAYS HAD A DIY ATTITUDE IN DEALING WITH THEIR MEDIA. Magazines provided the original information feed, and a handful of anemic titles kept skating alive at its low point. They were produced out of necessity, because skating has rarely been covered in mainstream magazines except as a novelty. It was the low-budget videos, though, that acted as the nuclear weapons of exposure. With music, editing, and cinematography, they create skate parts that can blow up a skater and a company overnight. And a more commercial documentary, such as *Dogtown and Z-Boys*, can do the unthinkable: get today's skate rats to ponder the past.

A TWO-PAGE PHOTO OF A HORSE JUMPING A ROCK

Lance Mountain: I was in seventh grade, in '78, when skateboarding took a major turn for me. There was a big difference in the magazines from the year before, when there had still been lots of handstands and leg lifts in them.

It didn't matter what the magazines tried to push on me—I knew what I liked. [Tony] Alva, Stacy [Peralta], [Jerry] Valdez, [Kent] Senator, [Tom] Inouye, [Chris] Stropple—they did everything rad. I didn't like the ones who had mustaches doing the gymnastics stuff. My friend appreciated all aspects of skateboarding. He'd look at a magazine and say, "Ty Page is good!"

I just saw a visual: "He's got a uniform on. Can he really be good?"

SkateBoarder magazine turned into Action Now [the first action-sports magazine] in 1980, and that made me realize skating was dead. Billy Ruff won a contest as an amateur and got a full-page photo. [Christian] Hosoi won the second contest and got a full page. I won the third contest, and naturally I thought I'd get a full-page photo. I opened the magazine up, and there was a two-page photo of a horse jumping a rock. Skateboarding was over. It was a bummer.

The way Thrasher looked [when it was first published, in 1981] was depressing. It was newsprint. I wanted a color centerfold to hang on my wall. But it was our magazine. It was our deal. It was us. Thrasher laid it down: Here's what skating is, here's what it's about—follow it. Whether you like it or not, Thrasher says, "We dictate what skateboarding is."

Transworld's motivation was, "Well, we don't like what Thrasher is saying, so we have to do something different." Transworld had good photos, but it didn't stand for anything.

Thrasher and Transworld were there to promote this thing that didn't exist, to make it up. The backyard-ramp contests were put in the magazines to pretend that this scene was happening, to make it happen.

EVERYBODY STARTED MAKING IT HAPPEN FOR THEMSELVES

Tommy Guerrero: Thrasher helped pull everybody back into the fold in the early '80s. They created the community, letting skaters know that there were other people out there doing it. That's what it comes down to—looking for some people of the same ilk, compatriots, brotherhood. The attitude of the founders was just like kids. They were going to the punk shows and were like, "Fuck everything—we'll do it ourselves."

Thrasher's events brought skaters around again, guys like the Meekster or Stevie [Caballero], people I hadn't seen since the parks closed—I started seeing them again at the contests, or whatever little event was going on. You'd keep in touch, and they'd say, "Come to San Jose and skate my ramp." Everybody started making it happen for themselves.

HAVING A PART IN A POWELL PERALTA VIDEO WAS GOING TO MAKE ME THE STAR I WANTED TO BE

<u>Mike</u> <u>Vallely</u>: Before I saw the magazine, somebody told me I had to check out *Thrasher* magazine. I had never heard the word before, but I understood it the second I heard it. *Thrasher* in the mid-'80s really captured the essence of skating. The first one I flipped through had Natas Kaupas on the cover, and it was called the Street Sequence issue. I had known people skated bowls, but this was skaters using their environment to create, and that spoke to me. My perspective opened up. I was totally alive just from seeing those photos.

Transworld had better paper and all-color photographs, but *Thrasher* was skateboarding to me. The whole spirit of the magazine was very much in line with where I was coming from and my approach to skateboarding. It was some kind of conduit between me and my heroes and me and my dreams.

Later, I got sponsored by Powell and got the cover of *Thrasher* and won amateur contests, but it all felt like preparation for my own part in a Powell Peralta video. Having a part in a Powell video trumped magazine coverage, contests, everything. I knew when I watched *Future Primitive* and *Animal Chin* that I'd watch them for the rest of my life. I'm telling you, Stacy Peralta nailed it.

Those early videos were timeless. Having a part in a Powell Peralta video was going to make me the star I wanted to be and would cement me in skateboard history. I knew the opportunity that was in front of me, and I wanted to make the most of it. My expectations were immense.

After filming my part, I had a sinking feeling. I didn't feel that it had gone the way I wanted it to go. I don't remember discussing anything with Stacy [*Peralta*]. They filmed it and left, and then I went to the premiere.

At the premiere, halfway through my part, nobody had clapped or cheered. Everything started swirling around, and I felt nauseous. My dream had been to be featured in a Powell Peralta video, and it wasn't playing out like I had dreamed it.

I think my part stands the test of time, for sure, but I think there was a moment where I was the best street skater on the planet, and I wanted my part to tell that story. When I talk about these things, it sounds like I'm bad-mouthing Stacy Peralta, which is difficult, because he's probably the most important skateboarder of all time, in my mind. It was Stacy's vision of skateboarding that I related to most. But my relationship with him was very strange. I didn't get along with him, and I think I was a source of anguish and stress for him.

People were so complimentary about the video part. They enjoyed my skating and were moved and inspired by it. But at the same time, I knew I was better and it could have been bigger. It was a strange paradox.

I'D NEVER SHOW IT TO MY FAMILY. SO AWFUL...TERRIBLE.

<u>Stacy</u> <u>Peralta</u>: *Freewheelin'* [*released 1976*]...absolutely terrible. It was night-marish when it came out. Not only is the story bad, but they had a guy score music to it, and he made up all these goofy skateboard lyrics in the music: "I'm just

Craig Stecyk and Stacy Peralta filming an inverted Tony Hawk, Del Mar, 1984. **Photo:** Grant Brittain

STALEFISH

flowing with you, da-dah-dad-dah...." It took Broadway tunes and applied them to skateboarding.

And then *Skateboard Madness* [*released 1980*] was so bad that my parents even commented to me, "Wow! Did you know it was going to be that bad?"

[*Bad mainstream skate films*] don't do anything and don't help anybody. Nonskaters don't pay any attention to them. They couldn't care less, because it's bad filmmaking. It doesn't please anybody. I can't look at that stuff. I'd never show it to my family. So awful...terrible.

AFTER FILMING TONY HAWK FOR THE FIRST VIDEO, I TOLD HIM, "THIS NEXT YEAR, YOU HAVE THE ABILITY TO WIN EVERY SINGLE EVENT." HE BLEW ME AWAY THAT DAY, JUST KNOCKED ME OUT.

I had already made one little skateboard video in 1982. It wasn't even a video— just a ten-minute thing. We sold three, or something like that. It was before home VCRs were invented. We sold it to some skate shops, because they had the ability to play them.

In '83, D. David [*Morin*] was living next door in Hollywood and was taking a film class. He and a filmmaker friend had done some pieces for the Christian Broadcasting Network and did one on Mike McGill, who was Catholic or something. One day, D. David said, "Dan and I will make you a skateboard video for 5,000 bucks. Why don't you pitch it to George [*Powell*]?"

George and I thought it was a good idea. I didn't realize there'd be a home market for videos, because VCRs were just coming in, so we made it for stores. Stores were starting to have media areas as a way to attract kids, showing surf movies, but there were no skate movies.

D. David was also an actor, and the first day he couldn't make the shoot because of a TV job. I went instead and didn't get along with the crew he'd put together. Lance [*Mountain*] and Steve [*Caballero*] didn't like them either, so I fired them and took over. I just started renting cameras and shooting. I didn't know how to do anything. We had started spending money, so we had to get it done.

When I started cutting that first video, George and Craig [*Stecyk*] and I were sitting around watching it and said, "This section of Lance skating to places is really cool. Why don't we make that the way to tie the whole thing together?"

It took me six months to edit, and eight months for everything: shooting, editing, getting the music. We didn't show strictly skating. We wanted to mess with it a little bit, make it fun.

We premiered *Bones Brigade Video Show* in Tony Hawk's living room after a Del Mar contest. Surf films were made for auditoriums, and skateboarding videos were made for living rooms. It was apropos that we premiered it in a living room—that's ultimately where it was going to be played.

Everybody chuckled when Lance was skating and Eddie Ratigue came on camera. The skaters watching the video loved it, but nobody had any idea it was going to sell 30,000 copies, or however many it did. The impact was so strong that we were getting calls from skateboard-distribution companies across the world. The Australian distributor called us and begged us to do another video. "You must do a video every year, because these videos are helping grow the sport. You have to realize that for every kid who buys one, 100 are seeing it, and every one of them will buy skateboards."

Lance had a personality that allowed us to expose him. Caballero, McGill, even Tony at the time didn't necessarily have an on-camera personality. Later, Tommy did to a certain extent. Lance is a clown. He was able to open himself up on camera and show how weak he is. He showed that even though he's good, he's like everybody else, he's normal. That endeared him to people: This guy's a kook, just like me deep down. Aside from Frankie Hill, Lance ruled the slam section in our videos. And when Lance fell, he not only fell, he fell in the funniest, the most endearing way.

Lance was never presented with an ego. Lance's whole thing was crushing the ego. That's why people liked him so much—he was not afraid of looking stupid. People would take their guard down when they watched him and say, "I want to do that. He's just having fun. He's not Joe Pro." He does embody the fun of it.

After filming Tony Hawk for the first video, I told him, "This next year, you have the ability to win every single event." He blew me away that day, just knocked me out. He was so inventive, doing tricks like fingerflips and airwalks in the air—stuff that no one had ever thought of.

He was not well liked by the Northern California crew, which was *Thrasher*, and they controlled the media at that time. He wasn't hardcore, he wasn't a punk, and they looked at him as an upstart and were threatened, because Tony threatened their stable of skaters who held down the old guard. Tony was part of something else.

It was the skateboard videos, in my opinion, that really showed the world what Tony was capable of. We did an end-run around the magazines: "OK, if you're not going to show Tony, we're going to show him ourselves, and we're going to show him in a better way, where you can actually see what he's doing." People finally realized, *Man, there's* nobody *doing what this guy is doing.*

One of the things we had that you didn't see in other videos was cutaway shots to other skaters reacting to the maneuvers. Incorporating the scene and the excitement of being there into the video was really important. It was *super*-important. I just felt that the spirit was really important. I heard that some college professor up at Stanford encouraged his class to watch *Future Primitive*, our second video: "If you want to understand California culture, look at this video."

I did get a letter complaining about a swear word on a wall: "Couldn't you have shot around that?"

THERE'S ANOTHER AVENUE TO CREATE THAT LEVEL OF RESPECT

Bob Burnquist: Videos showed me another side of skateboarding, and after that all we wanted to do was film. We'd all skate and film and then watch the video later. Videos changed the importance of contests—before, to get sponsored or go pro, you had to be good at contests, but now you could create a following with a good video part. It doesn't matter if Danny [*Way*] ever wins a contest again. There's another avenue to create that level of respect.

VIDEOS CHANGED THE IMPORTANCE OF CONTESTS—BEFORE, TO GET SPONSORED OR GO PRO, YOU HAD TO BE GOOD AT CONTESTS, BUT NOW YOU COULD CREATE A FOLLOWING WITH A GOOD VIDEO PART.

Videos create a different type of pressure, because the expectations are higher for every new video, and to keep ahead of that is really, really hard—but it's a lot more creative than creating a contest line.

SOME PEOPLE JUST SKATE FOR FUN, YOU KNOW?

Daewon Song: Videos were and still are the most powerful thing—it's judgment. There are people who get first in every contest and can't get a sponsor. Your whole career is based off a video part. If you have a bad video part, kids think you're a bad skater.

Chris Cole is a gnarly skateboarder, and if he said, "Hey, kids, I'm going to stop doing video parts," they'd be like, "I don't care if you're winning any contests—we want to see some proof." It's a way to live up to your name if you're a professional skateboarder who is progressing.

Chris [*Haslam*] and I always skate mini ramp, and we decided to do a video together, and that's how *Cheese & Crackers* came about. Mini ramps have always been one of the funnest things to skate, stuck in the middle between vert and street. The motivation for the video was for people to watch it and go skate mini ramps and have fun. Some videos are too 'core. Some people just skate for fun, you know? They watch a slam section and see these kids almost killing themselves, and it's not going to motivate them to skate. But if they see a fun video, they're like, "Dude—yes! *That's* why I skateboard."

IT WAS A SHITTY WAREHOUSE, A FORMER METH LAB WITH DEAD RATS

Chris Haslam: The atmosphere of the warehouse where *Cheese & Crackers* was filmed was purposefully done. Daewon was a dirty skate rat, and that's what I was— it's what we still are, pretty much. We love that shit. We wanted a grungy, dirty look

1   *Cheese & Crackers* video cover. **Photo:** Courtesy of Dwindle Dist.

2   **Daewon Song** calculating the fun derived from a mini ramp, former meth lab, 2006. **Photo:** Courtesy of Dwindle Dist.

to the video. It was a shitty warehouse, a former meth lab with dead rats—even the ramp, which started out good, turned shitty because of all the holes we wore in it. We told the owners not to clean anything, because it reflected what we are. That's how skating was when we were growing up, right? I wish it were still like that. We did spray-paint the walls, even though we weren't supposed to.

It took three months to film. We'd skate every day. It was stressful but awesome at the same time. We wanted to make it legit, and were really nervous before the video came out—fifteen minutes on the same ramp? If some dude skated the same rail for fifteen minutes, it'd be like, *Come on.* …I didn't know how people would take the goofy tricks like the tire-rolling deal, but it was fun to do, so whatever.

The response was insane. Skaters talked about liking the whole vibe, the tricks, the atmosphere. They thought it was hilarious. At first I thought they were kidding—some stuff was corny, but people loved it. Even the dudes who I thought would hate it because it was mini ramp were pumped on it.

THE FILM TOUCHED ON CHASING A DREAM AND BEING TOLD YOU'RE A PILE OF CRAP

Stacy Peralta: The most rewarding thing about *Dogtown and Z-Boys* was seeing how many middle-aged men it reawoke. They reinstituted skateboarding into their lives. And I'm one of those guys. A lot of these guys thought, *I have the wife, the kids, the job, the house—but I want to [experience] that feeling again. I want to remember that I'm part of this great tribe.*

I got a letter from Europe that said, "I was sexually abused as a child, and skateboarding was my only outlet. I've never been able to talk about it and deal with it, and when I saw this film, it set me free."

The film touched on chasing a dream and being told you're a pile of crap. And then achieving the dream and being told, "You know, you're not a pile of crap, and what you're doing is amazing."

If I go to a party and people ask what I do, I say I'm a documentary filmmaker. I get the same response that I used to get when I said I was a professional skateboarder. If I said I was a feature filmmaker, it'd be a different story, but I say I'm a documentarian, and it elicits very little interest. It stings, but I'm used to it. I know the terrain from skateboarding.

CONTESTS

SKATERS OFTEN DISMISS CONTESTS AS A MEASURING TOOL, CALLING JUDGING TOO SUBJECTIVE TO ASSESS TECHNICAL DIFFICULTY, SPEED, AGGRESSIVENESS, AND STYLE. They also harshly judge contest organizers and their motivations. A raw event in a skatepark across the street from a strip joint packs much more impact in the skate world than a slick televised one does.

The value of contests has fluctuated wildly since their inception over thirty years ago, another sign skateboarding will never comply with the conventions of traditional sports. The contest run that may best capture skateboarding is Neil Blender's 1985 street-style run where he made advanced liptricks look easy, rolled on the ground with his board between his legs like an interpretive dancer, launched an awesome tweaked air and slowly raised his fist in mock cele-bration, and ended by spray-painting a nervous-looking face on a wall.

Tommy Guerrero, car hop, Capitola, 1984. **Photo:** Grant Brittain

<u>Steve Olson</u>: I don't know my first contest. I'm trying to think of that…no…not really…I don't remember my first skateboard contest.

I HAD BEEN DUPED—BY MYSELF!

<u>Rodney Mullen</u>: The last professional freestyle contest was in Savannah, Georgia, in 1991. I so wanted contests to be over. I'd held that title [*world champion*] for a long time [*ten years*], and I wanted it to end. It was exhausting. You can't get out, and I wanted it to end. I won't even play checkers anymore, because I never want to compete.

I don't even remember Savannah being a contest—for me the last one was San Francisco, before that. I walked around after that contest. The area was so messy. And I was thinking about all my *Rocky* years of late nights, and all the miles I used to run and all the stuff I used to do to uphold this "title." My big lofty goal, my title of titles: to win ten years of contests. After my sixth year of winning, I thought a whole decade would be cool. I made such a huge thing of it. I thought the sky would open up. I thought I'd have peace or nirvana or something. There'd be enlightenment. All those years…I can't believe what an idiot I was. There was no closure. I had been duped—by myself!

No one gives a rat's ass about stats in skateboarding, which is the beauty of it. I imposed it on there, and that's where I got out of control and backfired.

The world is surrounded by me-against-you, and a consistent thread in skating is that there are a lot of people who want to escape that. Even when they're put in a competitive situation, they don't even conform to that, and it becomes a bit of a joke. We've all been to football games, baseball games, tennis matches, and they're very organized. You go to a skateboard contest and the judges are getting *high*.

That's the nature of a team in skateboarding, which is really cool—what is your unique contribution? You get ahead by being different, by being yourself, not by copying someone.

In some ways, contests are bigger than ever before—the purses are higher, there are more of them, more publicized, on TV—but they're less important than they ever were in the culture.

WITH GREAT POWER COMES GREAT RESPONSIBILITY

<u>Russ Howell</u>: Larry Stevenson, owner of Makaha skateboards and inventor of the kicktail, organized the first skateboard contest in 1963, in the South Bay of coastal Los Angeles County. And then the first national contest was held at what was then Anaheim Stadium in 1965. My friends and I tried to bike to the contest, which was twenty miles away. We got lost in an orange grove and missed it.

The Del Mar Nationals in 1975 were sort of a testing ground for skateboarding. The event was a huge two-day contest with more than 500 competitors from all over the nation. There were no significant skate stars at the Del Mar contest. No skater had an advantage due to their name within the sport, and the open contest offered no distinction between amateur and pro. Everybody competed in the same events, and no thought was given to the contest as being a "pro" event.

Rodney Mullen, something extremely technical and difficult, Carson, 1987. **Photo:** Grant Brittain

A few of us at Del Mar were in our mid-twenties, with over fifteen years of skating experience, and it was obvious that the old-school skaters from the '65 era had contest experience and did a lot better in a competitive format. The Dogtown kids were inexperienced with skate-contest formats.

There weren't very many rules. It was totally disorganized. For freestyle, you had two minutes and one skateboard to show what you could do on this flat platform. I was twenty-five at the time, and the Dogtown guys were thirteen and fourteen years old. I knew from gymnastics training that you had to plan your routine: a spectrum of tricks to maintain a degree of difficulty, and you didn't want to fall off. I was taking a gymnastics class and a dance class, so that influenced how I skated back then.

Winning the National Freestyle Contest opened up doors of opportunity to do skate demonstrations throughout Southern California and the world. My motivation to tour was always to spread my passion for skateboarding and to elevate the sport to the level that it deserved. I got a lot of tours off of that win, and I took it seriously. It was like that phrase in the *Spider-Man* movie: "With great power comes great responsibility."

THEY WERE GETTING THEIR TROPHIES, AND WE WERE GETTING OURS

Stacy Peralta: After the Bahne contest [*at Del Mar in 1975, where the Zephyr team debuted*], every month or so there would be a new contest, and they were only free-style and slalom. There was no such thing as competitive bank-riding or pool-riding contests. And there was no sanctioning body. It was like, "Oh, the world championships are next week." The next week, it was the state championships. The next week it was another championship.

But the contests were very important, because they were the only ways to get into *SkateBoarder* magazine, to keep your profile high, to land the big sponsorships. Getting paid to skateboard was a *dream*.

The whole time I was on Zephyr, I wasn't paid. Nobody was. In fact, the first professional contest happened right after the Zephyr team broke up. It was at the L.A. Sports Arena in 1976 and was called the Hang Ten World something, or whatever. From that point forward, people started winning money and getting their names on boards.

Before that contest, you entered your age group. There was a teen division, junior men's, and men's, and "pro" was sometimes just the "advanced" division. And there was a girls' division.

At that time, Tony [*Alva*] and I were in the junior men's division. We were the best. I hate to say this, but seriously, this was the truth. One day Henry Hester and Bob Fullburg [*who were in the men's division*] came up to Tony and me and asked, "How old are you guys?" We told them and they said, "Great! We have a year left."

We were kicking their ass in slalom. We were beating their times, but they were getting their trophies, and we were getting ours.

I DON'T CARE WHAT ANYBODY SAYS, IT'S STILL LITTLE LEAGUE

Steve Olson: The Zephyr team had their team uniform, which was jeans, blue shirts, and Vans. And the other teams had their weirdness. I don't care what anybody says, it's still Little League. Before, teams had their mesh jerseys and stuff, and then the pool thing came into it, and the jerseys and all that weren't quite as important. It got less formal with the pools. You're traveling with your team, and whether it's dysfunctional or not, it's still a team, and you're going to a competition.

SHE CALLED UP SANTA CRUZ AND LIT INTO THEM

David Hackett: I was fifteen and an amateur in the 1975 Hang Ten contest. The first *SkateBoarder* ran an ad for the Skateboard Racing Association: "Join Now! $10." I grew up in Malibu with a lot of hills, and I was the fastest skateboarder I knew of, from bombing them every day. So I joined the Skateboarding Racing Association and sent in my $10, and they sent me a sticker, a T-shirt, and an entry form for their first sanctioned event—the 1975 Hang Ten World contest at the Los Angeles Coliseum.

I was shocked when I went to the contest. There were teams and banners and ropes, officials and people with suits and clipboards, and announcers and spotlights and all this shit. I'd had no idea that there was an industry.

Looking at the freestyle competition, I was definitely in over my head. They held the slalom and downhill on a portable wooden ramp that Bahne had endorsed. It was about forty feet long and raised on one end to a height of about twenty feet on an angle of maybe three degrees—pussyville.

The cross-country course was about ten to twelve feet wide in some areas, like the start, then narrowed as you hit these little banks and carved hard and fast around three or four cones placed on top of the banks. You could push the whole time but not hit any cones or veer off the course. Jay Adams won our age division.

I rode a homemade board I'd made in wood shop at Malibu Park Junior High School. The Santa Cruz guys had better equipment, and I probably ended up winning because they left. They thought the qualifying was the finals and saw the trophies on the table and thought, *Oh, these must be ours.* So they took them and left.

I stayed at the contest and won, and I didn't get a trophy. I was pissed. My mom never supported my skateboarding, but goddammit, if somebody fucked with one of her kids, she was going to kick some ass. She called up Santa Cruz and lit into them. They sent my trophy back and ran a retraction ad in *SkateBoarder* magazine.

I didn't go to the 1976 Hang Ten contest after I had won my event in '75. Isn't that lame? I didn't even know about it until I read about it in the magazine afterward. Mostly, I'd hear about future contests at the contest I was at: "Next week is the Marina Del Rey Dogbowl contest. Be sure to be there!"

I'd be like, "Huh? I want to go."

TO DO MY BEST AND NOT TO EXPECT ANYTHING

Steve Alba: It was '78 and I was fifteen, and my mom was concerned about me going away by myself to the Spring Valley contest [*the first professional pool riding contest*]. I was driving with another pro skater and this older man who owned one of the companies that sponsored me. My mom agreed to it and told me to do my best and not to expect anything. On the drive, these guys are drinking Heinekens, smoking weed, snorting coke. I was in the backseat, clueless. I knew what beer and weed were, but I was like, *What are those guys putting in their nose?*

I was just a pup, and I didn't understand the politics of the skateboard industry. I was amateur until Tunnel Skateboards told me I was going to enter the contest as a pro. I became friends with a lot of the other skaters later on, but at first Stacy [*Peralta*] and Jay Adams were the only two dudes out of all the pros who would come and say hi to me. Alva was so arrogant—and gnarly.

I WAS FIFTEEN GOING ON SIXTEEN, AND I GOT $3,500 FROM WINNINGS...BY THE TIME I WAS SEVENTEEN, I HAD ALMOST EIGHTY GRAND IN THE BANK.

I think I won because I had this endurance no one else had. It was a two-minute run and judged on every wall, and I had more walls than anybody. I was the only guy who could stay in the pool the whole time. I won $1,000.

They had all these side events, like who could do the most one-wheelers, and dudes would lay down on the deck to make sure the wheel went over the lip. They also had a pipe-pasting contest where you would stick a sticker up as high as you could.

I came back home with a check, a bottle of champagne, and around ten boxes of products. All these companies wanted me to ride for them. I ended up riding for G&S for the second pro pool contest in '78. I only rode for them for that one contest, because they sucked after a while, and then I rode for Alva. Alva had been lame to me at first, but he was the best dude then, and on top of that, they were willing to pay me $500 a month. I was already getting paid $50 a month from Krypto wheels, and Indy paid me. For a fifteen-year-old kid still in school, that was a lot of money, so I signed a year's contract.

I got photo incentives from Krypto: $100 for a quarter-page photo, $250 for a full page, $1,000 for a cover. Then I made my sponsors match my winnings. When I won Big O in '79, I was fifteen going on sixteen, and I got $3,500 from winnings and matchings. By the time I was seventeen, I had almost eighty grand in the bank.

1   **Steve Alba**, Big O, 1978. **Photo:** James Cassimus
2   **Tony Hawk** and trophies, 1986. **Photo:** Grant Brittain

POOLS SEEM TO BE MAKING A BIG STINK IN SKATEBOARDING

Steve Olson: I won the first pool contest, straight out. It was an amateur one at Concrete Wave, before Spring Valley. That was '77, and then the Hester series happened later on. I jumped on Santa Cruz and turned pro for them. They said, "We need this dude, because he can ride pools, and pools seem to be making a big stink in skateboarding." They had slalom dudes, Henry Hester, but there was no such thing as a pro pool rider yet.

Santa Cruz just said, "There's a pro pool contest in Spring Valley. You're going pro, and we'll pay you this much money."

I was like, "Really? Sweet."

I remember exactly how much I was getting, but I can't really voice that answer—it's too pathetic. I'd never thought about getting paid to ride a skateboard. I was sixteen, and suddenly you were getting paid and you were like, *Fucking what? Sweet!*

OK, I got $200 a week.

It was sick having pool contests [*instead of only freestyle and slalom*]. *All right, a pool contest! Now we can skate like in real life.* I liked skating all the other things, too. There were some sick freestyle guys who ripped back then who were way more fluid. They drew lines and actually had to think about their routines. But there was a total emphasis on pools. Period. All the attention went straight to pools.

I was learning tricks in my run at Spring Valley. I did a carve and pushed it into fakie. I got third. Then Upland was after Spring Valley. I got fourth, and Salba, who had been expected to win, fucked up and didn't do good.

THAT WAS A BUMMER TO HEAR

Tony Hawk: Contests, for a time, were the only way for people to gauge who they thought was the best, and that changed once videos became more common. There were some people who were way more into contests than other skaters. Christian [*Hosoi*] and I were, for sure, but Jeff Phillips just thought it was a funny event. He wore a homemade shirt at an Upland contest that said, "I will try to survive Upland."

Around 1985, if you won an event, you'd probably get a picture in a magazine and a ranking. Getting in the magazines was the only other way to get recognized, because videos were very limited. To get in skate mags, you had to do something extraordinary—some amazing new move, or going higher than anybody had gone. Or you had to go on a skate trip with a writer and photographer, and those were rare for me. I was younger, still in school, and not a cool guy who was invited on trips.

I collected my trophies and put them in my room, but after a while I felt that it wasn't what I wanted to hold on to. I'd see pictures of people, not necessarily skaters, and they were in front of all their trophies, and I was like, *Who cares? You should be measured by your current abilities.* I wanted to keep proving myself, not think about how great I skated last year.

The trophies and rankings started to mean less to me. Once a contest was over, I looked ahead. I'd walk away from the podium and hand my trophy to someone or throw it into the crowd. In '87 I got burned out on contests, because the pressure was on me to win, and if I skated my best and liked my run but got second or third, people said, "Oh...he sucks now." And sometimes people just wanted another skater to win. I felt a little like an outsider to the other competitors. A few times skaters would tell me, "I hope I get second place, because you're going to win." That was a bummer to hear. I wanted to be a peer, not the standard.

I couldn't let contests mean so much, because it pained me. I know Rodney [*Mullen*] went through the same thing, and for him it was probably worse. Contests just were not fun, and I always enjoyed my skating, so I backed out of them for a while. It was hard back then, though, because it wasn't really possible to make a living if you didn't compete. I said I'd do demos, but my sponsors told me that the demand might not be there if I wasn't competing. Your contest results were how you were recognized back then.

After a few months, I eased back into competing with a different approach, and it became a lot easier. I just went for it, and if I landed everything, it was going to be way better than anything I'd done before in a contest. Or I was going to explode and blow out. It was more fun that way.

When I finally quit contests in '99, it was a huge relief. I wasn't a slave to the contest circuit. It was nice to be able to enjoy a skateboard contest, instead of retreating into myself and thinking about how I had to make this and land that. As much as people don't want to hear it, there is a strategy to competing in a skateboard contest, and I learned it pretty well.

CONTESTS ARE THE "JOB" PART OF WHAT I DO

Bob Burnquist: My first contest was in '89, when I was thirteen. You had to skate a mini ramp, vert, and a street course all in your run. Nobody else in my age division could skate vert, so I won. I came home with a trophy, all stoked, thinking, *This is easy!* I thought I was so cool.

My second contest was against amateurs with no age division. I had really bad asthma and could only hit four walls before running out of breath. I got thirty-second place. I was devastated, and my asthma was so bad that I couldn't even cry properly. I told my mom contests were stupid, and I wasn't going to enter them anymore.

My dad drove me to my third contest a few months later, and I skated it as if I didn't care. I bailed, laughed, goofed off. I didn't even check the results, and I liked that feeling, but my dad looked at me and said, "Don't ever ask me to take you to a contest again. I will never take you with that kind of attitude in life. If you don't want to be here, don't be here. You could have just gone to the park and skated." He was right.

Skaters are generally competitive with themselves and their expectations. If I put together a contest run the way I want to, then I'm fine with it. If the judges give the contest to someone else, then whatever, peace, I'm stoked. I've definitely evolved into this attitude—I used to get upset.

Bob Burnquist, very high and very switch, Vancouver, 1997. **Photo:** Grant Brittain

in, flaming lien to tail, Tahoe, 1985. **Photo:** Grant Brittain

I used to have a conflict with some contests when I wasn't paid to do them. But after I had my daughter, Lotus, and was making a living off of skating, I just dealt with it. Contests are the "job" part of what I do. It's that outside pressure that I don't like. I like the pressure I put on myself when I skate, but that's my own.

LET'S GO TO SOME KID'S HOUSE IN THE MIDDLE OF THE COUNTRY

Stacy Peralta: I was involved with Fausto [Vitello] on the first ramp contest, the first street contest, the first ramp contest in the middle of the country. He was always the guy who physically made it happen, but he and I and [Craig] Stecyk would talk about where to go next.

Other manufacturers had their heads up their asses. Skating was in a slump and they didn't bring anything to the table—all they did was follow. And we weren't following anymore. We were going to take the lead. The one great thing about Fausto is that he was a motorcycle rider with the heart of a street skater, and he remained that way to the end. He always wanted to make sure that we were being true to the sport.

The first ramp contest was in Palmdale, in Southern California in 1982. We could see ramps were where it was going. We had to get out of the arenas and go where the kids were doing it themselves. We started having these ramp jams in backyards, like Joe's Ramp Jam in San Leandro. Then we thought, *Let's go to some kid's house in the middle of the country.* We found a kid in Nebraska with a ramp, and we held a contest at his house.

It was all part of trying to present skateboarding in the most honorable and honest fashion. We were not sanctioned in arenas anymore—we were going right to the heart. It was going to be totally unorganized, totally Podunk, the absolute opposite of anything you'd ever see presented on television. You'd walk outside of the guy's backyard and be on a street, and there were kids on bicycles and skateboards. It was real skateboarders hanging out, sitting on roofs, fences, hanging on tree branches. Everybody was welcomed, nobody had to pay, nobody was told what or what not to do.

Lance [Mountain] convicted us of manipulating skateboarding at the time we put on the first street contest. "You guys are trying to make something happen that doesn't exist."

We kept telling him, "Streetstyle is going to exist. We've got to do this." And what happened? A year later Lance is a street skater, Cab is a street skater, and even Tony Hawk becomes a street skater. It was our business to see the future.

We kept the street-contest area dirty. Usually we spray-painted all the ramps to make them look bad, more street-oriented. If we got a car in there, we allowed the guys to bash it up, so there was that kind of experience.

Having a successful street contest legitimized a whole number of skaters that weren't being legitimized, like Tommy [Guerrero], Mark Gonzales, Natas Kaupas, Jesse Martinez. There were all these guys who were skateboarding but weren't doing what everybody else was doing. They were kind of like these oddities. This contest put the spotlight on them and said, "What they're doing is legitimate, and we have to pay attention."

The beauty of street skating was that it was more liberating than vertical, because you could do it anywhere. It didn't require a $1,500 wood ramp in your backyard. A kid living in an apartment could now aspire to be Tommy Guerrero or Mark Gonzales or Natas Kaupas.

WHERE'S MY LOOT?

Tommy Guerrero: I wasn't sure what the hell a "streetstyle" contest was. When they said it was going to be in Golden Gate Park, I was like, "What are they going to skate there?" But once you showed up and saw the parking blocks and little wedge ramps, you were like, OK. It really wasn't trying to mimic a street—it was sort of the best of trannie and street stuff. It was on a little hill, and you'd go down and hit the obstacles. I think one of the first obstacles was a parking block. I did an ollie-to-pivot to start my runs.

I wasn't even sponsored. I had been sponsored by A-Lot-a-Flex, a skate company from Berkeley, during the late '70s. We'd enter team contests and say, "We're not a team, we're a cult!" So I had entered contests before.

I JUST DIDN'T GET IT. I FIGURED IT WAS A $200 PURSE, AND WHOEVER WON WOULD GET IT. THE MONEY WAS MORE IMPORTANT THAN ACTUALLY WINNING...TWO HUNDRED BUCKS TO A KID WITH NOTHING? I WAS SEVENTEEN, AND I HAD DIRT.

I didn't really trip on the fact that I was competing against a lot of pros. In 1983, it didn't really mean too much to be pro. Skateboarding was so small, and these were all newer pros. It wasn't like it was Jay Adams and Tony Alva—it was Neil Blender and Billy Ruff and these cats we knew as vert skaters, and we hadn't been skating vert since the parks had closed. I'd been skating parking blocks.

I really didn't even understand the amateur/pro thing back then. I just entered because it would be a good time. It was definitely more like a session—skaters coming together and having a good time drinking beer, hanging out. It was pretty emotional when I found out I'd won. There was a $200 purse, but nothing was allotted for an amateur. I really didn't understand. I was pissed: "What the fuck? Where's my loot? Give me the loot!"

I just didn't get it. I figured it was a $200 purse, and whoever won would get it. The money was more important than actually winning. Fuck yeah, it was! Two hundred bucks to a kid with nothing? I was seventeen, and I had dirt. My mom raised my brother and me. She worked, but it was very tight. We moved in with my aunt and uncle several times, and there'd be ten of us in a two-bedroom flat. We had a great childhood, but there were times when it was a bit difficult. So two hundred bucks was serious loot for a little punker who's got nothing. I was really into playing bass [*in the punk band Free Beer*], and two hundred bucks meant I could get a real bass. They rectified it by giving me a complete setup—and that was like pulling teeth.

AS I TURNED PRO, I FELL APART

Mike Vallely: When I first started skating, in 1984, a contest was a fun way for people to show their skills and get together, nothing I took too seriously. It was the only way we knew to get people together and express our love of skating.

I think I won every sponsored amateur contest I entered, but as soon as I turned pro, I fell apart. I got third in my first pro contest, but by then my feelings about competitions had caught up. I knew I could skate in a pressure situation, but I didn't feel like I *had* to skate in a pressure situation. And the more pressure that got put on me by sponsors at contests, the more I felt like I had to perform. It no longer felt like that gathering. I never really was a top competitive skater again—that ended very early in my career.

WHOA, HOW CAN I BE THAT BAD?

Lance Mountain: Stacy asked me to ride and work for Powell in 1983, and the last professional contest where I rode for Variflex was at Kona. I did horribly. There were ten pros and an amateur who beat me. So I got eleventh in a contest that didn't even have eleven pros. I was pretty devastated after that contest. Even though I could not have cared less while I was skating, afterward I thought, *Whoa, how can I be that bad?*

Contests were just a good time to hang out with my friends, like [*John*] Lucero, and have fun. If I thought I could do good, then the contest kind of mattered, and if not, then whatever—I just goofed around. I'm like a brat and a teacher's pet—when I knew there were consequences, I could make myself do things I didn't want to. If first-place prize money is $100—I'm going to have fun. If first place is $10,000…then you know what? I'd better try.

Contests weren't all about winning. I really wanted to impress Stacy [*Peralta*] at the Great Desert Ramp Battle. I did an invert channel. It was just one trick—I don't even remember skating in the contest. My goal wasn't to win the contest; it was to stand out by showing this one trick that other people couldn't do.

It was brutal having a family while being a pro skater in the mid-'80s. I don't think anybody in the spotlight had done it before. At first you didn't really want to let anybody know, because it could make you look old and kill your popularity. But then I stepped it up and started doing good in contests.

My number-one thing was to provide for my family, and skateboarding was what I did. But I had to make a sacrifice, and some of the fun and carefree attitude kind of went out the door. I had to win contests and make a little money and prove myself, and that *was* work.

Part of being a professional is showing people how good you are. I knew competitions weren't about beating somebody else—they were about putting on the best show I could. If you win a contest at all costs, then you don't really win in skateboarding. I'm not a huge contest guy, and by my conversation you can tell I think contests are retarded. But if you can be the best in a video, go to a demo and kill it, enter a contest and get top three, be in every magazine doing new stuff, then you're better than everybody, because you have all those things covered.

Skateboarding, for me, is not work, but entering a halfpipe contest on the same ramp over and over, doing the same tricks—that's work. That's very sports-oriented to me. I'm not trying to be an X Games basher, but I have no interest in watching an X Games vert contest. It's like when my mom made me watch ice skating. They practice the routine the whole year; they go down the chute and flip-flop, flip-flop; and if they make it, they're number one. Just because somebody is good doesn't mean you have to like it.

Popular skaters make you want to be them, or part of what they're doing. That comes from personality, look, theatrics. Popularity within skating is based on theater, not sports. The only time people really use stats is when it gets out of skateboarding's hands and someone wants to make a business out of it.

The business of skateboarding is selling skateboards, and that is always going to be based on theatrics: Who makes people want to be part of their deal? Competition is about stats, and that's why there can be a huge gap between popularity and people who win contests. A lot of the guys who enter the X Games don't even have their own models.

The X Games are trying to get a handle on this and manipulating their contests into an invite-only format. But there's still a bunch of competitors who are unpopular within the skate world. And you can't make them popular by advertising—skaters are popular because people want to be them.

THEY DIDN'T GET THE CONCEPT OF TRUE SKATEBOARDING

Tony Hawk: There was a pretty severe learning curve for events like the X Games in the beginning. They wanted to make a made-for-TV event that lumped together skating and other fringe sports and label it "extreme." But they didn't look deeply into the personalities of each one. If you look at the street course from the first X Games, it looked like something out of the video game *720°*. Everything was pink or green, and everything was transition. They didn't get the concept of true skate-boarding. It was more about the aesthetics.

The Skatepark of Tampa is down and dirty, in a sketchy area of town. But skaters are used to those sketchy areas, because skateparks could only rent in places with the cheapest real estate. At its big annual contest, the announcers tell people to get the fuck off the course—that's the Skatepark of Tampa, it's for real. But people know who won the Tampa event, and they may not know who won the X Games. It holds the most importance in the skate industry. It's hugely important to have events that are by and for the skate community and not in conjunction with other sports. The Tampa contest is one of the few standards that remain.

Kevin Harris, kickflip, Vancouver, 1987. **Photo:** Grant Brittain

WE'RE DEAD!

<u>Kevin</u> <u>Harris</u>: Rodney Mullen's dominance helped kill competitive freestyle. The guy lost one contest in more than ten years, and even that loss was debatable. I could see how some people would think the contests were boring. Even if Rodney fell five times, he still deserved to win.

After a contest in 1990, I overheard organizers for the National Skateboarding Association discussing the new season of freestyle contests: "We probably shouldn't do any more freestyle contests, because Rodney wins them all, so what's the point? Why don't we just have the freestylers do demos at contests?"

I thought, *Holy shit—we're dead!* I realized that I would lose my community. A big part of the contests was being together with your friends, skating with them.

When I showed up at the arena for the 1991 Savannah contest, there was no room for a freestyle area. Instead they sent the freestylers off-site to this crappy area, a twenty-minute drive away. The only crowd was family, maybe 100 people at most. The big crowds were back at the arena watching ramp and street. The whole drive over, I was thinking about why we were being put aside like a second-rate circus act. It was insulting.

The skateboard industry was still huge in 1992, but it let us down. I just felt that the freestylers had done so much for the sport. We did more demos than anybody. We brought skateboarding to people who had never seen it before. On the other hand, I was exhausted from traveling for the previous eight years of my life and skating every day solid for the last fifteen years of my life. I was married and had a young son at home. But I missed that pressure of competing. I miss it to this day.

SKATERS CAN BE UNGRATEFUL TO THEIR FOREFATHERS.
Most tricks have expiration dates and get old and
stale. Techniques change and equipment evolves, making
it possible for the average skater to easily land
maneuvers that only the elite could pull off decades
earlier. Many new skaters, lacking perspective, assume
that their predecessors simply sucked. It's influence,
not age, that defines the generations in skateboarding.

In the late '70s, a generation lasted maybe three
years. In the early 1980s, a generation lasted almost
a decade. But however long it lasted, when a generation
was deemed "old school," it was instantly cast off.
Only recently have skaters started looking into their
past. Instead of laughing at the clothes and prehis-
toric equipment, they have begun appreciating the
pioneers and are even influenced by them.

I CAN SEE WHY OTHER PEOPLE INTERPRETED THAT AS WEIRD

Russ Howell: All the best skaters were at the 1976 World Invitational at Nassau Coliseum in New York. Every contest was independent, and they were usually hard-pressed for qualified judges. Often it was first-come, first-serve to whoever wanted to judge. You'd have four or five judges from one company on the bench. At this contest, people were so fed up with using [crooked] judges that they hung huge applause meters from the ceiling.

The total purse was $20,000. A three-way tie was awarded to me, Steve Cathey, and Gary Kocot for best showing. Torger Johnson came up to me after the results were announced and said, "You know, Howell, we all skated in this contest—you ought to split the money between everybody." Torger and I almost came to blows.

At a contest in 1977, I talked to the director about dispersing the judging responsibility: "If you look over at the table, you have four Logan people there, and they have cheated in other contests."

"Oh, no, they've given me their word," he said. Sure enough, a Logan rider won that contest. It was really obvious that so many people were getting burned.

Another altercation came at the 1977 Orange County Fair during the Southern California Skate Championships. Ty Page and I got into words with each other. I had heard he was bad-mouthing me, so I went over and, in the most Christian way I could, said, "Ty, you have your style, and I have mine. I respect yours, but you're talking about me, and if you continue doing that we're going to have problems." Later on that same year, we performed at a Munich Sports Show together and became great friends.

I don't skate the way I used to. I'm more of a surfer. I've gone back to my roots. I used to have more of a dance-routine [style]. I can see why other people interpreted that as weird.

WE WERE COCKY ENOUGH TO KNOW WE WERE WAY BETTER THAN THEM

Stacy Peralta: Steve Olson was stuck between two generations. His timing was, unfortunately, terrible. He was between the generation of Tony [Alva] and me and Tony Hawk and [Steve] Caballero, and his generation had a very brief life span, which is unfortunate, because Olson is such a great skater. He was in a transition time. [Brad] Bowen, Steve Alba, Duane Peters, all those guys—they all were in that transition time. They came after us but were more reflective of us than of what was coming down the line. By the time the new style came in, which was all in the air, they didn't have the goods.

The coping was our boundary line, in a sense. We could get a foot or two out in aerials, but that was it. In a tight pool, you can't launch—you don't have the speed. But on a ramp, if you mix the right transition with the invention of flat-bottom, all of a sudden you don't even need the ramp to do tricks on—you're using it to get into the air. From that point forward, it was all about getting out and in the air. Once they developed the ramp, the boundaries changed, and with that came a new style.

Steve Olson, Upland, 1985. **Photo:** Grant Brittain

1

3

2

1   **Steve Olson,** Vancouver, 1986. **Photo:** Grant Brittain
2   **Christian Hosoi,** Del Mar, 1985. **Photo:** Grant Brittain
3   **Dave Hackett,** Sacramento pool, 1989. **Photo:** Grant Brittain

Skaters don't have many aspects of their history in their lives. They don't get fed their history. I don't know if the magazines do much history in their editorial, so skaters don't have much access to it. And if they don't have the access, then they probably don't have a reason to pay attention to it.

In the early '70s, we knew that in the distant past there had been a Hobie team and a Makaha team, but to us they were a bunch of dinosaurs. We were cocky enough to know we were way better than them. If we had seen what they had to overcome to become as good as they were, then our appreciation would have been greater. We didn't have access to that information. If younger skaters had access to their history, I think they'd be totally interested in it, because it's other people doing what they love to do. Whether they respect it or not is another thing.

I WAS IN THE HALFPIPE THINKING, *WOW, NOW I'M GOING TO GET MY ASS BEAT.*

Steve Olson: In '77 and '78, there were generations of skaters that happened within eight months of one another. Salba won Spring Valley, and it was totally *on*. Kids were on fire. I was just sixteen, and then there were some of the competitors who were men, like twenty-four-year-olds—that's an eight-year difference. You're still in high school, and this other guy has maybe been divorced. But the older guys rocked.

I broke my ankle at a Big Bob Texas demo in '80, and it took me out of the whole scene. I think I was riding with Salba, and while I was doing a frontside carve, my ankle just went on me. I didn't even wipe out. I shot my board, and it went firing up and hit some big Samoan who was bending over the halfpipe to see what was happening. The board hit him in the head and he just fell back.

I was in the halfpipe thinking, *Wow, now I'm going to get my ass beat*. And then: *This is wack. Hey, what did I do to my ankle?* The guy came over and asked me to sign his board. "Absolutely, bro! I'm so sorry."

"It's cool. You're pro."

I was out for five months, and when I came back, skating's popularity was going down, but it was also progressing to the next place, which was up in the air. *Tricks* were happening: ollies, backside airs to axle stalls, footplants, inverts, Miller flips. Everyone passed me by. *Boom!* All these guys are going on to the next level.

Skateboarding progressed from kickturning and carving to tricks like rockwalks, fakies, fakie 360s, and then rock 'n' rolls came in, and then airs, and Bobby Valdez did an invert at Newark, the third Hester contest, and then the progression really just rocketed. [*Steve*] Caballero came in and was doing his thing, Eddie Elguera, and Duane Peters. A whole new generation of dudes came up through that downtime in '80.

Then I cracked my head open trying to learn how to ollie. I was way behind. My heart was totally not into skating. I wasn't skating at my level, and it was a little disheartening. And I didn't really like all the "tricks." I wasn't into the invert. It looked ghetto to me—grabbing between your legs, tickling your nuts while you're upside down? Big deal. I was more into the music scene and the way it looked, and I had started a band.

Skating was dying. It went quick. Skateparks closed and whatever…it was done. 1980 was worthless. Skateboarding was dying, and I felt sorry for everyone who hadn't gotten a piece of the action. Skateboarding gave me a life.

WHAT DO YOU THINK YOUR SENSEI WOULD SAY? HE WOULD SLAP YOU

Dave Hackett: I was getting bummed out on the whole competition thing. By late '79, shit was getting harder. Before that, the meat and potatoes of a vert- or pool-contest run would be a frontside grind, backside grind, tailtap, frontside air, back-side air—if you were lucky, a rock 'n' roll. And if you were really lucky, you had an invert. Guys were winning contests doing footplants and these other *tricks* that seemed so gay. *This isn't what shredding and ripping and surf skating is all about!* They were halfpiping the pool. They had no lines. When we competed, it was about the lines you drew, the speed you generated, the style….

I don't do tricks—I do maneuvers. A trick is something you can teach a dog or a pony to do. A move—what we did—is something that you learn over many, many years, like martial arts. You don't do *tricks* in martial arts. If you went to a karate class and said, "Hey! Check out this trick!" and did a spinning back kick, what do you think your sensei would say? He would slap you.

Eddie Elguera looked like a robot when he skated. For us, skateboarding was all about how you looked, which is pretty narcissistic and extremely vain, but it comes from surfing, and style was such an important part of surfing. It didn't matter what you did, as long as you looked good doing it.

The "trick thing" was a new era being ushered in, for sure. And it wasn't some-thing that I thought looked good and wanted to be a part of. I felt immediately old. Immediately. It was horrible. I was considered an old-timer at nineteen. I went underground, back to skateboarding empty backyard swimming pools and skating for myself. I was over it. I didn't want to play the trick game. I've always been a surf skater. Besides, I couldn't do a kneeslide. Still can't.

WE'RE FROM THE BADLANDS, MAN—WE'RE GNARLY AND WE'LL OUTSKATE ALL YOU GUYS

Steve Alba: There were so many rivalries and divisions within skating. In the 1970s, Dogtown was a serious, serious deal. After Dogtown, I think we, the Badlanders, were the next best guys. Then you had the Down South guys, like Steve Cathey and Pineapple and Dennis Martinez. All these different groups of dudes were eyeing each other, checking each other out, thinking, *What's this guy got that I don't have?*

It was territorial, but at the same time Pineapple came up from San Diego and wanted to know my story. That was cool.

The old Badlands guys used to say, "You have to grind every wall. You have to give it your all every wall. There's no setup trick."

There were certain elitist attitudes that went with regions. "We're from the Badlands, man—we're gnarly and we'll outskate all you guys." Just as Dogtown was dying, the Badlanders took over.

THERE HAS ALWAYS BEEN A DIVIDE BETWEEN SKATERS

Lance Mountain: This is so embarrassing....I never got to see Alva skate from '76 through '78, when I really wanted to see him. At the first pro pool contest at Spring Valley—Salba wins. I have photos of me skating right after that, and I'm on an Alva board painted over with a Badlands logo.

The crazy thing about the skatepark scene from the end of '78 to '80 is that there were around five generations crammed into that time frame. Salba won the first pro pool contest, but you never considered him first-generation—you almost considered him third-generation. I felt there was another generation after him with guys like [Eddie] Elguera. And then my generation came in behind them. But we were only a year younger than Salba—those generations were just rat-tat-tat-tat.

The generation break is based on the approach to skating and the influence, not age. If you looked at the old magazines in the '70s, it was Dogtown versus Down South, and they made a big issue out of it. At the beginning of the '80s, there was the whole Variflex versus Santa Cruz thing. Variflex made wheels, trucks, and boards, which never happened with any other company. Indy trucks were strong, and they disliked Variflex because they didn't ride Indys. I believe that's where the conflict truly began.

Variflex dudes were very progressive. Eddie Elguera was inventing all these new tricks and leading progression along with Duane Peters. They were both very trick-oriented skaters, and both very robotic—neither of them were old school, with surf-style. I don't care what anybody says—Duane and Eddie skate the same. They have the same robotic, trick-oriented style.

Duane made his skating into theater. He made antics out of it, which is all part of skateboarding. You don't know tricks—you know personalities. Duane put on theater when he skated, and it was exciting to watch. You never knew what he was going to do. Eddie skated great, but he just did tricks, and that's why people don't remember now. He influenced skaters who were progressive and trick-oriented, like Tony Hawk. Duane created a following.

I was in between Eddie and Duane. I wasn't really close to Eddie, and I liked the way Duane skated. But I became very loyal to Variflex, because I was at contests where people were spitting on Eddie. Fausto, his wife, Salba, and all those guys were booing Eddie, and I just thought, This is lame. This is all great skateboarding.

But there has always been a divide between skaters. The Hosoi and Hawk style argument [Tony did tricks, Hosoi did style] has been repeated and dictated to a lot of people after the fact. It was one period of time, '84 to '86, when two dudes broke out of the pack and were the elites. The people arguing made more out of it, because they were followers of one style or the other.

In the early '80s, when we were young, I remember disliking Tony [Hawk] a lot. A lot. And it was only because we felt threatened. Totally. We'd play it off and say we were into [Mike] Smith because he skated rad and wore sweaters. Tony had a thing on his helmet. "It's a trick bobble and it teaches him tricks," we joked. We knew he was developing, even at his young age, a type of skateboarding that we couldn't do. We'd say, "Oh, that kid can't skate." But we wouldn't even have bothered saying that unless we had seen that he was going to do things that nobody else could. He just wasn't at that level yet. When you see somebody who really can't skateboard, you don't take notice.

TO THIS DAY, THAT WAS ONE OF THE RADDEST THINGS I'VE SEEN

Steve Alba: I feel bad for Tony [Hawk], because he gets a bad rap sometimes from people like Duane [Peters] and me, here and there. When he was a kid, we just hated that [type of skating], not the guy. I never hated Tony Hawk. There was just a time when you felt threatened, because you were the dude, and that shit happens to everybody. It was just the nature of skating: progression.

I was blown away when he rode Upland in that contest and did a halfcab slider to fakie around the corner. I was like, "What the fuck did you just do? Are you kidding me?" To this day, that was one of the raddest things I've seen.

I REPRESENTED A CLEAN-CUT KID WHO DID FLIPPY-DIPPY TRICKS

Tony Hawk: Some of the older skaters hated my style when I turned pro in '82. They thought I was doing these circus tricks and that I didn't blast or grind gnarly. Christian [Hosoi] was blasting airs, and people respected that. I wanted to learn tricks—that's all I cared about. It didn't matter to me what the rest of skateboarding thought, because my friends, like Kevin Staab and Lester Kasai, thought it was cool. We didn't look like we were flowing and surfing, and that was the big insult for the older generations. It was hard to break that boundary.

I didn't live in L.A. and have to skate with the guys who didn't like my style. I wasn't under their constant ridicule where I skated. I'd read what they said about me in magazines, or hear stuff at events. In one magazine they wrote, "There's this kid, Tony Hawk, that's pretty good, but all he does is ollie into his airs, so it doesn't matter how he grabs." I thought, *What's wrong with that? Sweet, now I can grab all kinds of ways.*

Around '84 or '85, contests integrated people from all over the country. Before that, the skatepark-series contests were based in Southern California, and not a lot of Northern California dudes were coming down. Once the series got bigger and everybody was riding ramps, there was an integration of NorCal riders.

The NorCal versus SoCal thing started when those guys came to Del Mar and decided they didn't like me and were going to root against me and boo, because they wanted Christian to win. The irony, of course, is that Christian is a SoCal guy. He's from L.A. So initially, it wasn't a NorCal versus SoCal thing—they just liked Christian. They just saw Christian as having better style, going high—he represented a gnarlier edge, and I represented a clean-cut kid who did flippy-dippy tricks. Then it became all about breaking unification. You're an Indy guy or you're Santa Cruz, and you're *definitely* not a Tracker guy.

I'd never heard booing at a skateboard contest before. At the end of my run, people would throw shit into the pool. I couldn't figure it out. I'd never seen such hatred or vibing in skating, and I kind of took it personally. All the people from the Del Mar area decided that they wouldn't stand for people booing a skater, so they started rooting me on.

It was weird for Christian, too, because neither one of us thought of the other as "the enemy." We were competitors, for sure, but we'd also hang out together. All of a sudden, these people had chosen us as the icons for what kind of skater they were. They were rooting for style and who represents what. Then the *Thrasher* versus *Transworld* war flared up at the same time. You either read this magazine or that one, and that defined who you were. Until maybe five years ago, there was still a NorCal *Thrasher* attitude.

Today, skating is more segregated in terms of what kind of skater you are: a skatepark rider, a street skater, or a pool skater, or a jock, which would be a competitive skater. Today, you can go to a skatepark and you're accepted, no matter what you do. If you did a footplant ten years ago, people were like, "What are you doing? That's old stuff." Now if you do a footplant, people are like, "Dude, that is so sweet."

I THOUGHT I'D BE DONE BY TWENTY-FIVE

Daewon Song: The Internet changed everything. Kids know everything, and back then I wasn't even aware of videos or magazines—and that's the kind of stuff that helps you progress. The progression of skateboarding is twenty times quicker than it was ten years ago. You go to bed and you wake up the next day, and it's progressed and you're like, *Oh, my God...dude!* You never think it's going to move as fast as it does.

The new generation is scary. I love it. It puts a fire under my ass. These kids are nuts. I skate every day, and it's because I love it. I'll go to the Chino park at eight at night when it's freezing, and I wake up in the morning and think about what I'm going to skate. If I don't skate for a day, I get antsy. I'm a wreck. I'll be distracted. It's an addiction for me. I freak out. I have dreams about tricks that I think I could land. I still feel like a kid, even though I'm in my thirties.

Fifteen years ago, a pro who was twenty-five was unheard of. I thought I'd be done by twenty-five. I thought being pro would be fun for a couple of years. Now, I never wonder if my body will be able to take skating when I'm thirty-five—I just think, *I've got to learn some new shit!* Rodney is still doing tricks that everybody else can only dream about, and he's over forty. The dude is still progressing.

I think every generation of pros watched another generation coming up and thought, *OK, these are the new guys—but the progression is going to end.* I never thought somebody would kickflip twenty stairs. I never thought Danny Way and Burnquist would be doing their crazy stuff.

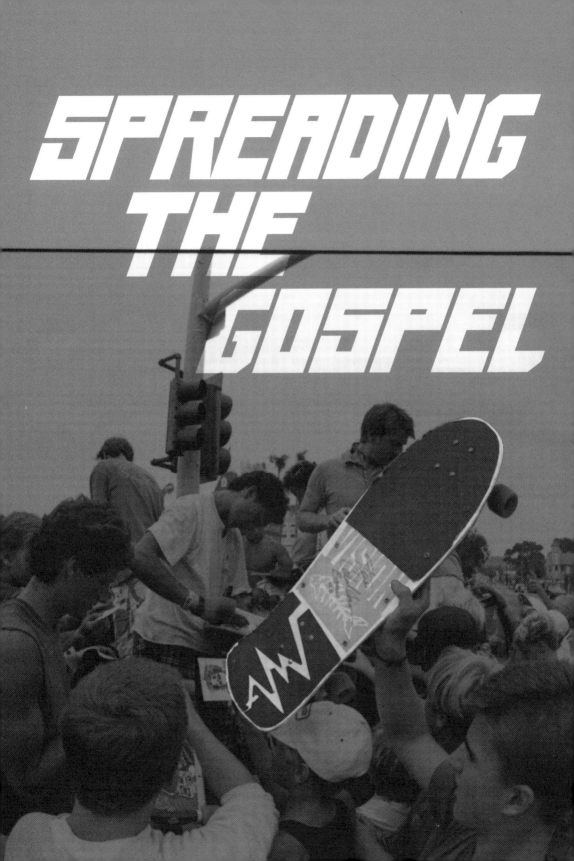

SURE, YOU CAN WATCH EVERY SKATER SHREDDING ON YOUTUBE, BUT NOTHING MAKES YOU WANT TO SKATE MORE THAN WATCHING A TALENTED SKATER SHRED IN REAL LIFE.

It's a testament to skateboarding that the most popular skaters can be met at a shop demo. Tony Hawk sells out stadiums and can also be found skating a demo at a random shop for a few hundred kids. Some skaters, like Mike Vallely, become addicted to the road and the personal interaction that only face-to-face skating can facilitate. He often breaks down the pro-skater barrier that can appear between him and average skaters by popping up unannounced at skate spots around the world.

THE GENDARME TOLD ME TO STOP IT

Jim Fitzpatrick: In '64, Makaha paid half of my $250 ticket to Europe to surf and gave me a dozen clay-wheel Makaha skateboards to take with me, saying, "Take these skateboards and ride them wherever you go, and if somebody is interested when you're done, give it to them."

I had my skateboard masking-taped to my carry-on bag, and when I got off the plane in Paris, I skated across the tarmac to the terminal. The gendarme told me to stop it. When I got into the terminal, I skated, and people freaked out. They were clapping, and kids would rush up. I did a demo in front of the airport while we were waiting for the charter bus, and 500 people were watching. My big tricks were two, maybe three 360s, tic-tacing around in a full circle, and doing the coffin, where you lay on your skateboard.

TODAY, IT WOULD BE CONSIDERED GOOFBALL AND CORNY

Steve Alba: In '77 there was a Pepsi skateboard team demo at my junior high school. Gregg Ayres, Rodd Saunders, and Stacy Peralta showed up to do it. The whole school gathered around the basketball courts to watch. Stacy did some 360s and walkovers, 360s on a bank ramp, and old-school kickflips, and they talked about wearing pads and your helmet.

Today, it would be considered goofball and corny, but in those days it was rad—Stacy Peralta was at our school! At the end, they introduced Mountain Dew to the school. They had all these tables with tons of little cups of Mountain Dew. I asked them to sign my magazines and said, "There's a pool down the street that I think you guys might want to ride. It's pretty dang good."

They actually went to these pools with us after school. At the end of the day, Stacy changed his wheels and gave me his old ones. I think they were Tunnel Rocks—one of the raddest wheels at that point.

THE FEDS HAD BEEN INFORMED THAT THERE WAS A HIJACKING POSSIBILITY

Steve Olson: In 1980 some skatepark owner dude, Big Bob, was having the Texas state championship or amateur state championship, and he was flying down thirty pro skaters. I think it was the first time that a bunch of pros went to one demo together. It was insane. Big Bob had said there was going to be a party at an all-girl dorm, we'd have our own hotel rooms, rental cars—it was going to be a blast: "I'm going to Texas. I don't have one person telling me what to do. We're just having fun."

There was no way the stewardesses could control twenty-five kids in a plane. The other passengers were wigging.

"We can't control them!"

"There goes another dinner roll flying past! Here comes some butter!"

"Look, a carton of milk!"

"Is that smell marijuana?"

There was lots of drinking. The captain came on the loudspeaker and announced that the authorities, the FAA, had been contacted and would be waiting for us in San Antonio, and we were in a lot of trouble. When we got off the plane, the Feds had been informed that there was a hijacking possibility. When they saw it was just a bunch of kids who were skateboarders, they just split.

We basically ran the contest and judged it, and Big Bob didn't have the girl party, didn't have hotels. He was full of shit, just some capitalist whatever. We didn't care.

THEY WERE SUPPOSED TO BE SETTING THE EXAMPLE!

Stacy Peralta: It might have been the first time that so many pros were together on a plane. People were throwing things at one another. Then Tom Inouye lit up a joint and took a few hits. The pilot said over the intercom, "Passengers, I'm sorry, but we have an element in the plane that is out of control. We are going to deal with it when we land. I don't think these travelers realize that this is a federal offense." Some federal guy gave us a serious talking-to when we landed. It could have been ugly.

Whenever skaters occupied the same hotel at contests, it would get trashed. What was funny was that even the older guys who worked for G&S, which was a very "straight" company, would end up drunk and going off the hook. They were supposed to be setting the example! At one contest in Newark, New Jersey, the hotel got so trashed that the hallway carpets were sopping wet. You were walking through inches of water.

I KNEW SKATING WASN'T OVER, BECAUSE I STILL WANTED TO SKATE

Lance Mountain: I was an amateur when I went on the Variflex tour in 1981, and it went on for over a month. I was with six other Variflex riders and Gil Losi and Mrs. Losi in one van. The older skaters had told me how amazing these skateparks were. Before we even took off, Apple and Cherry Hill skatepark closed. Gone. Another one in Texas closed down while we were on the way there. We went to Mobile, Alabama, for the Skate Wave, and it had also just closed while we were on the road. The only places that had a little bit going on were Surf and Turf in Wisconsin and Cosmic Wave in Kalamazoo, Michigan. It felt like skateboarding was dying in front of you.

The Losi family was already talking about going into RC car racing, because skateboarding was dying off. I knew I was going to skateboard forever, and I knew that if I was still skateboarding then it'd still be alive. I remember thinking, *Trucks and wheels are going to be really hard to make—should I save some? How do you make wheels if they aren't available anymore? Do I melt wax down into coffee cans?*

All the other riders quit skating after the tour. All of them. But I knew skating wasn't over, because I still wanted to skate.

EIGHT-YEAR-OLD KIDS IN ADULT BODIES

Kevin Harris: On the first Powell Peralta tour, in '85, Lance [Mountain], [Steve] Cab, and I left from Santa Barbara for three weeks. We drove around in George [Powell]'s Country Squire station wagon. I did most of the driving, and I guess I was sort of in charge, but it was never really discussed. Powell gave me a company credit card, and I always had around a thousand dollars in cash for per diem meals and hotels. They'd wire me money when it ran out. I was twenty-three and made $150 per demo.

The demos could be great or suck—it all depended on how the shops advertised them. Skateboarding was still pretty dead, so we never skated in big venues. It was more like, "Here's my 1,000-square-foot retail store, and you can go skate in the parking lot." Sometimes there wasn't any place to skate, and I skated on the carpet in pro shops.

By 1986, the Powell tour was stepped up a bit, compared to the previous year. I was paid an extra $150 a day to manage the tour. We still had the station wagon, but now we strapped a jump ramp on top. The demo areas were still mostly crap. Sometimes there'd be hundreds of kids crowded around the jump-ramp landing area. They'd pile in to see a skater pushing toward them, and once he hit the ramp and launched, they'd pull back. Not the safest thing to do.

By '87 we were insisting that the shops prepare for at least 1,000 people and use caution tape and banners to block off the crowd, as well as provide a shaded area for autograph signing.

We also had an official tour van. There was writing all over the seats and the ceiling. The outside was completely covered. During demos, you'd see the crowd writing all over the van. After a demo, it was like reading a bathroom wall.

The inside of the van was never clean. Every three days, I'd fill up a garbage bag with all the crap—bottles and chip bags, everything. Nobody ever took their crap out and put it in the garbage can. Bottles would be rolling all over the van, and the skaters were fine just getting back in and crawling all over their shit. Once we got on the interstate, I'd look in the rearview mirror and the skaters would be all crashed out with their Discmans on.

Sometimes it was like dealing with eight-year-old kids in adult bodies. By '86 and '87, these guys were making so much money. Their lives were chaperoned at that time—somebody always took care of them. If I tried to get them up by 9 a.m.—no kidding—it'd be at least 11:30 by the time we could leave. Two and a half hours to get four guys up and out of the hotel. And that's not with any breakfast.

By 1988 and '89, we had a portable mini ramp, and we had a crew of roadies for that. They would show up at the demo sites four hours before us and make sure everything was set up. Skating was booming. During our first year on tour, we averaged crowds of 300. The next year it was 800, the next year was 1,200, and the next year was 1,600. By '89 they couldn't hold them in skate-shop parking lots anymore. They'd have to close off entire parking lots.

1 **Tommy Guerrero**, San Francisco, 1987. **Photo:** Grant Brittain

2 **Adrian Demain, Tommy Guerrero, Steve Caballero,** and **Kevin Harris,** demo, Carlsbad, 1986. **Photo:** Grant Brittain

We had to pull to that thing down for every demo, and it must have weighed 150 pounds. Rodney did the free-style, and we jump-ramped until our backs gave out. —Tommy Guerrero

In 1990, skating's sales were going down fast. I called up for a summer tour schedule, and the team manager just said, "We aren't doing U.S. summer tours anymore." But then they just sent me on demos, and somebody else took care of all of us. That was fun.

Chris Haslam: On my first trip to California to skate with Daewon, I was picked up at the airport by the manager. It was sort of a tryout for the team. He said, "Oh, you're not going to make it as a pro skater. You actually made your flight. Pro skaters never make their flights."

NEXT THING YOU KNOW, VALLELY'S BALLS ARE TOTALLY ON FIRE

Tommy Guerrero: My first tour [in 1986] was driving around in George's souped-up station wagon, the Country Squire. I just remember driving with Rodney [Mullen] through the rain at four in the morning, in the middle of nowhere, lost. We'd gone in the wrong direction for hours, and we were discussing religion or the existence of a soul or things of that nature. It's pouring rain, there's a lightning storm, and we're lost in the middle of the South somewhere, driving a station wagon with a giant jump ramp strapped on top.

We had to pull that thing down for every demo, and it must have weighed 150 pounds. Rodney did the freestyle, and we jump-ramped until our backs gave out. More often than not, the surfaces you had to skate on were the worst. I'd look at the shop owners, the guys throwing the demo, and ask myself, *Do you skateboard? I'm not sure you do. I'm not sure you can ride on gravel.* It was brutal. Sometimes the obstacle was a four-by-four: "Go shred it!"

Then a few years later, the van came around with obstacles in it and on top of it for demos. It had a big jumper on top, some slider bars—but it was all Tetris in the back, and one guy would sleep on the box.

It was funky as hell, of course. I remember Lance peeing in Gatorade bottles, saying, "Oh, I overflowed!" Great. But for the most part, being the Powell kooks we were, we weren't too bad. It was totally fun, but kind of grueling. One time we were jump-ramping and Jimmy [Thiebaud] spiked the board, and it bounced back up and cut his nutsack open. He went and got stitches, and the next day it was "Get out there, kid. Throw yourself around."

But it was basically a rock-star lifestyle. You'd probably get thirty wake-up calls in the morning. With guys like Kevin [Harris], I'd feel bad, because he's the nicest guy on Earth and I didn't want to give him a hard time—but I'm telling you, I'm not getting up yet. There was probably some sort of troubleshooting going on, where he'd get us up an extra two hours early, and we knew that.

As long as you did your gig, you were fine and could do whatever you wanted. At home, I'd stay up late and sleep in and go skate all day. And if I didn't want to skate, I didn't, no big deal. On tour, you're getting up early every day and driving eight, ten fucking hours to go jump-ramp at a demo.

THAT'S WHAT HAPPENS WHEN YOU'RE BORED IN THE BACK OF THE VAN, TRYING TO GET TO A DEMO. COMPLETELY IMMATURE...AND YOU'RE JUMPING AROUND BEATING EACH OTHER UP, FIGHTING, WRESTLING. THEN THE BETS..."I'LL EAT AN ASHTRAY FULL OF THIS, THIS, AND THIS FOR X AMOUNT OF DOLLARS."

A lot of the time, you're just goofing off in the back of the van. Jimmy and I were king of the Tiger Balm—we'd use it for ankles, knees, everything. Jimmy wrapped his ankles with duct tape every single day and cut it off at the end of the demo. [*Mike*] Vallely was new on tour and not hip to Tiger Balm.

"What's that for?" he asked. "It gets hot?"

"Yeah, it gets hot as hell."

"No, it doesn't."

"Dude, it does."

"Fuck that—I'll put that on my balls."

"Go ahead. We dare you."

Next thing you know, Vallely's balls are totally on fire. "Dude, I need to wash my balls! My balls!" He's trying to rub it off, and we're telling him that's going to make it worse, cracking up.

That's what happens when you're bored in the back of the van, trying to get to a demo. Completely immature. Then you get to the hotel, and you're jumping around beating each other up, fighting, wrestling. Then the bets..."I'll eat an ashtray full of this, this, and this for X amount of dollars."

I was always like, "*You* are retarded. You guys are so bored." That's what they do in suburbia, because they're so bored. That's how *Jackass* and that shit comes about—boredom. Growing up in the city, there's always tons of shit to do. I was always, "I'm going to go over *there*, not doing *that*."

"SON OF A BITCH!"

Tony Hawk: I did a demo in Brazil for Powell in '88. It was with Lance [*Mountain*], and I ended up getting food poisoning, and began puking and shitting for two days. But a lot of people had come there to see me skate, and the organizers made me travel from my hotel room and announce to around 4,000 people that I couldn't skate.

The crowd thought I was bullshitting. Everybody started chanting in Portuguese. I didn't know what they were saying, but they were passionate about it. I kept asking what they were saying, and the organizer was trying to pretend he didn't hear me. Finally, he said, "Oh, nothing, don't worry about it."

I asked someone else, and they told me that they were chanting, "Son of a bitch!"

I was literally shaking, and my apology was the maximum time I could spend away from the bathroom. After pissing the crowd off, I ran to the bathroom and held a trash can in front of my mouth as I sat on the toilet. Then they sent me to a sketchy doctor's house, and he gave me some shots, and I passed out in this guy's house. I don't even know if he was a doctor—he just had shots. When I woke up, I felt better, and I skated the second day of the event. I felt like I was out of my head, delirious, but I skated and everything just clicked. I was floating around and did all my tricks.

After the demo, I felt these involuntary muscle contractions with my face, and they pulled my mouth up into this evil grin. I learned later that the doctor had used dirty needles that caused the lockjaw.

Powell took care of everything on those demos. When Birdhouse was going, in early '92, I had to organize the tours, which essentially meant calling up shops that carried our boards, which was not a long list, and making the travel route on a map. The first year we just used my own van, and the price for a demo was $400. I'd say we got paid two-thirds of the time. In New York, the guy just took us out for Chinese food.

If it worked out, we'd get $400 and I'd give $100 each to whatever pros we had, usually two or three. We all shared a hotel room—five dudes. You'd get two beds and take the mattress off the box spring, and two guys would sleep on a mattress, and if you wanted to sleep alone, you got the box spring, which was always my choice. As a company, we didn't make any money on those tours. It was about promoting our new brand. Skating was so dead that if we had 100 people show up, we were hyped. We'd eat at Taco Bell, Subway…well, that was it: Taco Bell and Subway. Those tours were a blast.

TAKING IT
TO THE
STREETS

DURING THE EARLY-'80S SKATE DEPRESSION, AFTER ALL BUT A FEW OF THE SKATEPARKS HAD DIED, MILLIONS OF SKATEBOARDERS DITCHED THEIR RIDES. But the lack of prescribed terrain opened up possibilities in urban landscape, and the stragglers found new places to skate. Skaters will employ any technique to acclimatize to terrain, and no style of skateboarding embraced that challenge with more creativity than street skating.

Early on, skateboarding looked to ballet, ice skating, surfing, snow skiing, and gymnastics as influences. In the mid-'70s, the rowdier skate rats scurried under fences and shredded backyard pools and schoolyard banks. That aggressive attitude was fully realized when '80s street skaters brought an urban-guerrilla mentality to skateboarding.

Once they started utilizing Rodney Mullen's flatland ollie, "obstacles" transformed into something to be ridden. Strapping on pads and finding a ramp was a hassle, and the purely flat-ground plane of freestyle appeared rather limp. The tricks that freestylers and vert riders spend decades developing were cannibalized for the streets, and this new style devoured their popularity.

IF YOU WERE GOING TO BE JUMPING BARRELS, THERE WAS A
RISK OF INJURY

Russ Howell: The typical contest in the mid-'70s still maintained the two old competitive arenas from the mid-'60s: freestyle and slalom. The freestyle routine was on a flat area, usually with no props. During the mid-'70s, you could use multiple boards for tricks. The routines were three minutes long.

The first cross-country contest that I saw was at the L.A. Sports Arena in 1977, and it was really cool. It was the first time I saw all the competitors come together and have a good time. Barrel jumping was only introduced in 1977, at the Long Beach Free Former contest. They had barrel jumping, freestyle, high jump, highest wall ride, 360 event, and slalom. There were only a few people who would enter barrel jumping. I think the only name you'd recognize would be Tony Alva. If you were going to be jumping barrels, there was a risk of injury. It wasn't worth risking a broken ankle on a barrel jump.

THEY LOOKED AT RODNEY MULLEN AND THEY LOOKED AT TONY HAWK AND
ASKED, "WHICH GUY IS HAVING MORE FUN?"

Stacy Peralta: You have to go back to the invention of the skateboard to understand freestyle. Skateboards, in their first incarnation [in the 1950s], were so primitive that you couldn't do hard turns or ride vertical, because the wheels were like rocks, and you'd slide out as if you had landed on ice. But you could go straight and do acrobatic tricks. Freestyle was the birth of skateboarding. You could do handstands or a nose wheelie or a tail wheelie or tic-tacs, the popular tricks back then.

In the early '70s, we figured out how to ride banks with clay wheels, but you couldn't do any maneuvers. When the urethane wheel came in, it allowed us to ride banks the way we had imagined, and we started doing moves like Bertlemann turns. When we went to the Del Mar contest in 1975, it was the first time that we'd ever seen [traditional] freestyle, and to us it looked antique. It had been invented ten years earlier, and to us looked like an old-fashioned way to skate. But in order to compete, all of us had to learn that stuff. There were only two types of contests: freestyle and slalom. Once in a while, they'd throw in cross-country or barrel jumping or high jumping as a sideline.

We took what the older freestylers did and hybridized it to make it more radical. I took the two-foot nose wheelie into a circle and spun 360s at the end and wrapped 360s into space walks. I enjoyed skateboarding anything, period, but I don't think a lot of the other guys enjoyed freestyle.

It wasn't until the [Henry] Hester pool contests in '78 that freestyle went downhill. And slalom, too. There was all this talk before: "You can't have a vertical contest. It'll never work. You can't judge objectively." The Hester series proved that we could have a pool contest, and that's what skaters wanted. People stopped freestyling because they stopped needing to freestyle. Freestyle was cool in the '60s because there was nothing to compare it against. Once pool riding was invented, nothing could be as cool as that.

But when we traveled the world in the mid-to-late '70s, the only kind of demos we could do were freestyle. You didn't show up in Australia with a ramp set up for you. There weren't skateparks.

Later on, in the '80s, when kids came into the sport, they looked at Rodney Mullen and they looked at Tony Hawk and asked, "Which guy is having more fun?" And clearly, Tony looks like he's having more fun. Freestyling attracted a very small percentage of skaters.

You could always tell a freestyler by sight. Freestylers do know who they are and have no qualms about it. If a guy street skates, he can still take his board to a park, ride it in a pool, on a ramp. When you freestyle, you can't do anything with that board except freestyle. It's really specialized. It's small. It's narrow. It has little trucks and little wheels. It barely works as transportation. If you're going to freestyle, man, you really have to love it, because you're not going to be doing anything else.

As a company owner, I never made money off of freestyle. I put Kevin Harris on the team in '82, and I didn't need him. I felt sorry for him. He was such a talented skater. I thought, *If I don't put this guy on the team, nobody is going to support him.* I could see how much heart he put into it, and Kevin is one of the greatest skateboarders in the world. Period. He becomes one with his board, and that's the greatest compliment you can give any skater.

I believed in freestyle. I felt it was a necessary art form, and even though maybe only 5 percent of the kids freestyled in the '80s, I wanted to keep it alive. If you look at what Rodney Mullen did, keeping him in the mix was so important. Rodney laid down so much of the foundation for modern street skating.

I think there's a place for freestyle in skating's future. It's a beautiful form. Every generation takes from the past and hybridizes it into something new. What's going to happen when we leave the age of extremism? You can only go so high and so far before you run into the ceiling of physics. So what's next? What's next is that skaters will take something done twenty years ago and put it together with something modern, and it'll create something unimagined.

Kevin Harris is a classic freestyler and represents the greatest aspect of '60s freestyle. He does it the best it's ever been done. The new hybridization could be a Kevin Harris on steroids. I once saw Rodney do perpetual 360s. He'd wind himself up and wind himself down with total control. What he was doing may not happen again for another twenty or thirty years, but someday it will be reapplied.

IT PAID OFF IN THE LONG RUN

Kevin Harris: In 1979, I got a registration form with the prerequisites for a freestyle contest that included a strength move. Out of the 100 total points, 20 depended on a strength move, like a handstand or V-sit. I was way too skinny to press up into a handstand from my board. I tried it for months, but I realized I'd have to lift weights for a year to do it. I eventually did it the weakling way, with a "beard sweeper," where you jammed your elbows into your stomach and used that leverage to lift your feet off your board.

I knew it was lame, and not because I was too wimpy to do it. It was totally gymnastics. I hated being forced to put tricks in my run that I didn't want to do—it seemed so opposite to what skating meant to me, being forced and told to do something.

By the mid-'80s, it was obvious that freestyle was the least popular form of skating, compared to vert and street skating. Stacy offered me a street board in the late '80s, but I just wanted a freestyle board. I felt that I would be selling out freestyle, even though I'd make more money. As freestylers, we always knew we were different. In the '80s, when street and vert skaters got together, hotel rooms were trashed, and what were freestylers doing? Probably watching TV in their rooms.

But it paid off in the long run—look how many freestylers own companies: eS, Etnies, Emerica, Birdhouse, World Industries, and Eastern Skate Supply were all started by freestylers. We fared better post–skate career than most vert skaters did.

WE *WERE* NERDS

Rodney Mullen: The reputation that freestylers had for being nerds was because we *were* nerds. I think it has a lot to do with the attention freestylers pay to detail. It would take *so* long to set up a freestyle board. You had to line the tips of the board with screws, put the plastic skid plate underneath, count washers, and shave different aspects of the board, because they were never right after production.

...FREESTYLE WAS CLOSING OFF. IT WAS A NATURAL PROGRESSION FOR FREE-STYLE TO DIE...STREET SKATERS WERE DOING FREESTYLE TRICKS WITH A NEW FREEDOM AND LOOSENESS. THEY TOOK THE VERY BEST OF WHAT FREESTYLE HAD TO OFFER.

I remember feeling that I didn't want to be as much a part of freestyle by '87. It was really closing off, and I couldn't ever see it moving forward. It wasn't that big of a deal when freestyle contests ended in '91, having been superseded by demos. The blessing of freestyle was that you didn't need any space, so it was the best type of skating for demos at the time. But within the skate community, where you really want the respect, you no longer had an outlet. How else were you going to get in the magazines when contests were over? With an occasional article, maybe?

By '89, you started to see some of the possibilities with street skating. Mind you, in its infant stages, it was really embarrassing. But there were some really gifted guys coming up, and through them you could definitely see where street skating was going—and that freestyle was closing off. It was a natural progression for freestyle to die. You have to ask: When does something become superfluous? Street skaters were doing freestyle tricks with a new freedom and looseness. They took the very best of what freestyle had to offer.

In '92, when Mike Ternansky said he wanted me to start street skating for Plan B, I tried to talk him out of it. I said, "This is a mistake. I will let you down, and that's a fact. I can't pick up what these guys on the team are doing."

I did it because he believed in me. Oh…it was hard. I'd try to skate a bench and plow right into it. [*Rodney had no skate depth perception from a lifetime of skating flat, obstacle-free surfaces.*] I learned noseblunts, and I did 300 in one night or whatever, and wrecked my knee. I trained militantly. There was *no* way I'd skate with people. It was so embarrassing. Talk about swallowing pride. I fought Ternansky the whole way through. I was a novice. Pathetic level.

Finally, I got a couple of tricks in the first *Plan B* video that weren't rotten, and that pushed me. By the next video, I felt I could really contribute, and some of the older street skaters would say, "You made up kickflips," so there was a teeny bit of grandfather respect from that. But I didn't feel like a real part of skateboarding until relatively recently, not until Enjoi started in 2000. The *Transworld* thing [*readers' poll award for best street skater*] in 2002 validated things, but it tripped me out. I had no idea.

ANYWHERE, ANYTIME, ANYPLACE THERE IS CONCRETE

Stacy Peralta: Street skating killed freestyle—straight-out. It even overtook the mighty vertical skating—who would have thought? Streetstyle was not only created from the skaters themselves, but from the industry. Fausto [*Vitello*], Craig [*Stecyk*], George [*Powell*], and I realized that we're selling all these boards to kids, and maybe 20 percent of them have access to vertical terrain. We had to start reaching the kids and doing something that reflects who they are. We started promoting streetstyle contests in '83.

When street skating first started, we weren't sure what it was. Was it jump ramps? Was it guys doing tricks on cars? The things that every street skater seemed to start with were the ollie and the ollie flip. Those two fundamental tricks are freestyle tricks.

Street skating began to hybridize what it could from vertical skateboarding, and certainly from what came out of Rodney Mullen freestyle—not the freestyle skating of the '60s. Rodney invented modern freestyle skateboarding. What he did on a skateboard had almost nothing to do with what they were doing in the '60s.

Tony [*Hawk*], [*Steve*] Cab, and Christian [*Hosoi*]—those guys took off in the '80s where we left off. They were the architects of what became modern pool riding. We rode the walls and lip and finally got out of the pool, and they took it to riding

1   **Rodney Mullen**, freestyle, Del Mar, 1985. **Photo:** Grant Brittain
2   **Rodney Mullen**, streetstyle, secret ditch, 2005. **Photo:** Grant Brittain
3   **Lance Mountain**, streetstyle, Houston, 1985. **Photo:** Grant Brittain

STALEFISH

the air. But up until 1985, skateboarders still had a '70s aesthetic. It wasn't until street riding came along in the late '80s that skateboarding, in my opinion, really became what it is. Street skating really defines what skateboarding is—it brought it back to its original state, which is anywhere, anytime, anyplace there is concrete. You don't need to build it, you don't need to design it. You can ride on a handrail, on a stair, on a curb—anywhere. Any kid can do it.

Street skaters were the first to embrace rap music. The vertical skaters originally were the ones to embrace punk music. Street skaters were connected to the urban sound and the urban feel and the urban look. They were the first guys to wear baggy pants. They removed the helmets and pads, and skaters stopped wearing shorts and instead began wearing long pants.

This drove it away from the surfing aesthetic, which was based around trunks. Removing the pads and helmets and wearing normal everyday clothes unlocked a freedom that had been temporarily lost during the late '70s boom, when everything briefly went into parks.

Street skating opened up ethnicity in a huge way. It made it possible for impoverished inner-city kids to skate, because all they needed was a skateboard and the surrounding architecture. That to me was the final disassociation from surfing.

If you look at skateboarding today, it is so urban and ethnic—it completely left its surfing roots and found itself.

I WASN'T PERCEIVED AS JUST A SKATEBOARDER ANYMORE

Lance Mountain: In the early '80s, Gonz used to come skate my ramp, and we didn't know his name. We thought he was just a kid who seemed like he wanted attention but couldn't skateboard. One day I dropped him off at the bus stop and watched him ride down the street. He didn't freestyle—he was riding the street the way you ride a pool. It made me think, *I want to do that.*

I realized that street skating was going to be bigger than vert in 1986, when I got sent around the country in George [*Powell*]'s station wagon with a jump ramp strapped to the roof to skate at shops. We were supposed to show people how to fly off a jump ramp, which was basically what we did at skateparks over fences because it was funny, and now it was professional skateboarding.

But there was a difference between what we did while street skating and what skaters like Mark Gonzales or Tommy [*Guerrero*] did—like ollies, for example. Look at *Animal Chin*—all the vert guys are trying to learn how to ollie. I tried to ollie the Gonz gap in that video, and I didn't even hit my tail. I tried to do it with speed! I liked street skating, though. If I didn't, I wouldn't have done it. Street skating is skateboarding to me.

But then I became a "vert pro" in people's minds, instead of a skateboarder. In the early '90s, Sal Barbier told somebody that I was a useless skater, and that's when it really hit me that I wasn't perceived as just a skateboarder anymore. And Sal was a top [*street*] pro who I thought was great.

LOOK AT A VERT ROSTER OF THE TOP TWENTY SKATERS—HALF OF THEM DON'T HAVE BOARD SPONSORS

Tony Hawk: Vert skating is more of a spectator sport than street skating, and so you don't necessarily get enough appreciation to make a living within the skate industry. But you have other opportunities—there are plenty of demos and tours that need ramp skaters. Even if it's a demo in a parking lot at a concert, then that's what you have to do to scrape by. There's more opportunity to perform publicly, or you have to go the competitive route, but generally you're not relying on your skate sponsors as income. Look at a vert roster of the top twenty skaters—half of them don't have board sponsors, but they have a Red Bull helmet. You can't be a vert skater and just skate your local ramp and get coverage and make a living. At some point, vert skaters either have to do something giant or super-tech, or go out and tour and enter contests.

I don't think vert skaters have a different mentality than street skaters—there are just different opportunities. There are plenty of street skaters who can make a living skating the way they want to, as long as they get coverage. Andrew Reynolds is heralded as one of the best street skaters, because he has the skills and gets the footage. A lot of skaters don't realize how it works, and vert skaters are sometimes thought of as jocks.

SKATING IS ABOUT CHASING THE FEELING OF NEWNESS

Bob Burnquist: By 1995, vert was already getting into second-class citizenship compared to street. I was just as much a street skater as a vert skater back then. I loved how Julian [Stranger] and [John] Cardiel just skated everything and anything. It wasn't like, "Now I'm just a vert pro." I'm just a skateboarder—let's go skate. I liked that mentality.

Nowadays, on a skateboard team, you have one token vert skater. There are no Vertical Assassins board brands, with all vert skaters.

I look at skateboarding as a big octopus. Mega is a tentacle, and the street tentacle is thick because so many people are doing it—but it's all skateboarding, and it can grow in different directions. It really is about keeping your mind open. That's why I build my different ramps. My vert ramp cost around $100,000, and the cork-screw ramp was $20,000, and the loop was around $15,000.

I think I've gotten good reactions with my [one-of-a-kind] ramps when it's purely skateboarding. I got a mixed reaction with the Grand Canyon thing [Bob grinded a huge rail into the canyon and base-jumped], because it involved something other than skating—base-jumping, with the mega ramp with a huge rail. That one was inspired by the Danny [Way] Great Wall of China jump and how strong that was. I wanted to get people off their couches, in a way. Vert skating has that "wow!" role for people who don't skate. With the TV exposure that vert gets, it lures people into skateboarding and gets parents to agree to get their kid a skateboard.

Skating is about chasing the feeling of newness that I had when I learned how to drop in. You learn that the way to keep that feeling is by learning a new trick.

It's an addiction. You can't feel that way unless you do something completely new, and at this point in my life, for me to feel that, it takes grinding into the Grand Canyon. It takes a lot more to get it.

I have so many ideas of obstacles and ramps in my head. I have the skills to do things that I can't build, because it's too expensive. Danny and I talk about this all the time: "If I made Kobe [*Bryant*] money, I wouldn't have cars and diamonds—you'd see the craziest, wackiest ramps."

IT'S ALL AWESOME

Chris Haslam: Freestyle was already dead when I really got into skating. When I met Rodney [*Mullen*] and saw Kevin [*Harris*] skate, I was blown away. I'd never seen freestyle like that in real life before. The space walking and the spinning and one-footed 360s? The dude did something like 1,000 two-board 360s! [*Kevin spun 1,032.*] When I saw those one-footed 360s....Man, I want to learn that, and I can't. That shit is so hard.

I want Rodney to teach me freestyle, but he refuses. If Rodney came out with a full bonus part of freestyle, people would shit their pants. It's been a long enough time from when people hated freestyle. I try to get him to do it, but I think he gets nervous about how people might take it. That shit is awesome. It's skating. Who cares if it's vert with pads or freestyle or somebody skating a handrail? I like seeing different stuff. I think people get psyched on seeing new things.

I don't like the hating part of skateboarding right now, where people say freestyle is terrible and vert sucks. Who cares if you're wearing pads? I've been trying to learn McTwists on whatever is steep enough. Remember when Tony [*Hawk*] did a McTwist in a street contest? That was awesome. If you take away the labels, it's all awesome. I'd love to be able to do a McTwist in a street contest.

IT HURT. I DIDN'T KNOW WHERE MY PLACE IN SKATING WAS ANYMORE

Kevin Harris: Most new kids don't know freestyle ever existed. If I skate at a park with my son, skaters come up and say, "Oh, my God—he's doing that Rodney Mullen shit!" They get stoked, but nobody calls it freestyle.

For pretty much a decade after freestyle died, it was not cool to do it around skateboarders. If I skated freestyle at a public skatepark, the vibe was, *Get the hell out of here*. I'd get heckled all the time: "Get with the program!" "Learn how to ollie!" It hurt. I didn't know where my place in skating was anymore. If I wanted to skate, I'd find a quiet place with no one around.

It's funny, because Rodney killed freestyle, and he was the one who brought it back. He started doing more of it in videos, incorporating it more into his street skating, and the kids loved it. It rules for me to go to a skatepark nowadays. Kids are all over it—they want to learn tricks, because it's so completely different. And there's a level of respect now, younger skaters thanking me for being part of the scene years ago. Now, the gnarliest guys in the park are some of the first standing next to me, asking me to show them tricks. Right now is the most fun for me.

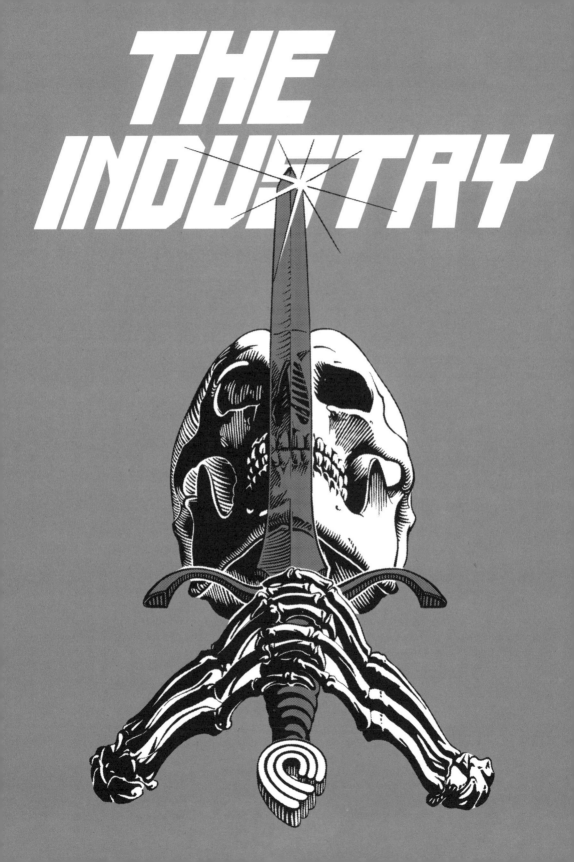

IN THE 1970S, MOST SKATE COMPANIES WERE RUN BY SURFERS OR SUITS TRYING TO HOOK THEIR CAPITALIST VACUUM UP TO THE LUCRATIVE SKATEBOARD MARKET. Tony Alva and Stacy Peralta, two former Z-Boys skaters, broke the mold when they started their own companies at the end of the '70s. They proved that a pro's "skate career" wasn't automatically severed when his popularity dwindled.

But the transition has been bumpy for many skate superstars who suddenly find themselves pushing paper and dealing with younger versions of their former selves as they manage a skate team.

IT WAS THIS POLITICAL MANEUVER THAT STUNNED EVERYBODY

<u>Jim Fitzpatrick</u>: Between 1964 and 1965, Hobie started making skateboards. Dave and Steve Hilton's dad, the Hilton Hotel guy, realized that his sons were accomplished skateboarders, and this was a big deal. He owned Vita Pakt, the orange-juice company that supplied the hotel chain with juice, and he joined up with Hobie. Dave and Steve left the Makaha skateboard team and jumped to Hobie. It was this political maneuver that stunned everybody: *Holy shit! These hot skateboarders from our team are now on another team!* We had rivals for the first time, and the whole picture changed.

The Hobie skateboard team stayed at the newly opened Hilton Village in Oahu, Hawaii. They were doing scheduled demos for the guests. Larry Stevenson, the owner of Makaha, panicked and had the team manager, Jimmy Ganzer, take his team to Hawaii. They were staying at this budget hotel, and Ganzer was young and in Hawaii by himself with an expense account, and he told the team, guys like Torger Johnson and Woody Woodward, who are all twelve, fourteen, fifteen years old, "I'm going down to the bar. Order whatever you want from room service."

Of course, drinks were ordered—that was the beginning of the end of the Makaha team. In 1966 and '67, skateboarding just came to a screeching halt. Everybody who wanted a skateboard had bought one, and a lot of them found out that it's not that easy and can be painful—and it's not wearing out, so I don't have to buy another one.

WE ARE MARKETING TO A POPULATION OF REBELLIOUS YOUTH

<u>Russ Howell</u>: Many of the skate manufacturers would gather together at the Hobie office in 1976 to discuss the direction we thought the sport should take. I voiced the opinion that certain ads were promoting the drug culture and that it reflected poorly on the sport. The majority of manufacturers replied, "Look, we have to do that. We are marketing to a population of rebellious youth. If we don't advertise to that market, our product sales will die."

I thought we had a responsibility to the people we were selling to. The meetings went on for about six months. It seemed like everybody was going to do whatever was right in their own eyes anyway.

THAT'S KIND OF SICK, ISN'T IT?

<u>Stacy Peralta</u>: I knew that I wanted to be involved with skating, and I wasn't going to let it go and do something else. Skateboarding was the world that I lived in, and I didn't want to leave that world because my time was up as a professional. But I didn't have role models ahead of me, and I had to figure out how to make it happen.

I thought about this a lot while I was still a professional. I chased it and talked about it for about eight months, and when I made my decision, very few people understood it. [*Stacy quit G&S after two years.*] I knew my days as a professional were numbered. I took a huge pay cut, but I was buying into a future. I had an instinct about George [*Powell*], and it was a right one. I was creating a new life for myself within skateboarding.

I have to give credit to Tony [*Alva*], because his company started that concept of doing it differently. But his ads were image-based with esoteric pictures—I wanted to do stuff with humor and satire, create an identity that skateboarders could realize. There was a way to create ads that reflected more of what I felt was a true skateboard identity.

SKATEBOARDING WAS THE WORLD THAT I LIVED IN, AND I DIDN'T WANT TO LEAVE THAT WORLD BECAUSE MY TIME WAS UP AS A PROFESSIONAL.

I can't tell you how many times the team riders would say, "Can't we just have an ad where we're skateboarding?"

Craig [*Stecyk*] and I would say, "No. If you want a picture skateboarding in a magazine then get in the editorial, but we're not doing it in our advertising." We wanted the advertisements for ideas, image—they weren't for skateboarding.

Bones came from Bones wheels. George had developed white skateboard wheels, and it seemed obvious to call them Bones. One day I was with Stecyk, in '78, and I said I didn't want the "Powell Peralta Skateboard Team." There had been the Sims team, the G&S team, the Logan team—I didn't want that term in the vernacular of what we were doing.

Stecyk just said, "Bones Brigade."

I went, "Bingo, that's it. Done."

There was a tongue-and-cheek nature to the military aesthetic of the Brigade. When we put together the very first Bones Brigade shirt, which had a plane on the back, an insignia on the pocket, and bombs on the sleeve, people freaked. We showed up at a Del Mar contest, and it was a really big deal. Before that, you put the logos of companies on the back. To the best of my knowledge, it was the first skateboarding shirt that didn't have anything to do with skateboarding on it.

We were the first company to come out with colored skateboards. Nobody thought you could color skateboards—who would want to buy a colored skateboard? They're wood. And we did the first full-screened board ever.

Shortly thereafter Stecyk and I had a meeting with George, and we were looking at boards on a wall, and I said, "We cannot look at the bottom of skateboards as skateboards anymore—we have to look at them as a canvas. We have to be able to paint this canvas now. It's not a skateboard, it's a piece of art."

When we first came out with the Ray Bones graphic [*Skull and Sword, arguably the most recognized skateboard graphic*], people were like, "That's kind of sick, isn't it?"

I remember even asking my parents, "What do you think about this? Is this going too far?" V.C. Court had a style, and he did most of the graphics, and so we developed a look. It was based around skeletons and fine-line drawings. In the '80s, skulls were a big look, and we just happened to jump on it at the right time. Back then, trends lasted longer—we rode that for at least six years.

We started out as a nothing company, and in three years, I think, we were number one. We took over the mighty Sims and G&S. They were the giant companies back then, but they weren't reacting fast enough. They weren't doing what kids wanted. Because we were small and needed to take chances, we could be the leaders.

I'M A BUM, NOT A BUSINESSMAN

Lance Mountain: In 1983 it wasn't as if skaters had careers. We were still figuring out if "professional skateboarding" existed as a career. My goal was to never work and try to make a living off of skateboarding. It wasn't as if I expected to make a good living—I got on Powell making $200 a month, and I thought that was good. I just worked other jobs to get by.

A year and a half after I got on Powell, I got married and my board came out, and my checks were instantly two grand, which I could live on at that time. It was perfect to keep me skateboarding. The money built slowly from 1984 on. My royalty checks went up to four thousand, then back to two thousand, then back up to six. In 1986 or '87, my royalty checks went to ridiculous amounts, where I was making twenty grand a month. I think *Back to the Future* and *Animal Chin* set it off, and Powell also stepped up production. But that dropped drastically. It didn't wind itself down, and that's the thing that was crazy. There had been a big jump from seven grand up to ten, fifteen, and twenty grand—and then there was a big drop back to seven grand or five grand near the end of the '80s, and I could live on that. Then *boom*. It stayed a grand for six months, and that's when most of the older pro skaters on Powell left.

It wasn't that hard to leave. Something had to change, because we couldn't live on a grand a month. And it was easier, because I always felt that I rode for Stacy [*Peralta*], and I knew he was over being involved with Powell Peralta and going to leave. Tony [*Hawk*], Mike [*McGill*]—we didn't quit Powell; there was no option, because the company didn't support us enough to continue doing what we wanted to do, which was skate.

And to a certain extent, we were being told that we were old and nobody liked us anymore and good-bye. That's what you're told as a skateboarder when the magazines stop giving you as much coverage and the companies don't sell as many of your boards. It'd be nice if companies set up something for skaters who have contributed in the past and maybe paid them enough to keep skating and make a living, but maybe there isn't the money around for it.

Being a professional skater is all about cash flow. If you can live on a thousand dollars, then cool. But if you have to live on ten thousand dollars and the market can't support that, then you move on to something different. I never lived like I was

1

2

1   Lance Mountain, Baldy, 2003. **Photo:** Grant Brittain
2   Bones Brigade: Adrian Demain, Ray Underhill, Kevin Harris, Rodney Mullen, Per Welinder, Eric Sanderson, Steve Caballero, Tony Hawk, Mike McGill, and Lance Mountain, 1984. **Photo:** Grant Brittain

A real skateboarder is just somebody who just wants to skateboard and goes and does it...it's never what anybody behind a desk is telling you...

–Lance Mountain

making twenty grand a month, but I never thought skateboarding would lose it to a point that paying the mortgage and buying groceries and a car would be a problem.

I was told, "Your problem is that you're trying to support a family off of skateboarding, and skateboarders aren't supposed to have families." There's always a bit of defining what a "real" skateboarder is from companies. "A real skateboarder is supposed to live on the road and in the gutter and sleep in a tent, not hotels." A real skateboarder is just somebody who just wants to skateboard and goes and does it. That's a real skateboarder—it's never what anybody behind a desk is telling you, and it was harsh, because I became the guy behind the desk telling people what skateboarding was, which sucked. I knew that's what it would be like, and I hated it.

I had to move on, so I started a skateboard company in 1991. It was terrible. All of a sudden I was doing something I didn't want to do, which was work. Stacy was the guy who proved you could stay in skateboarding by working in the industry. When I couldn't live off of what Powell was paying, I just thought, *Yeah, this is what I'll do.*

There were parts of running the Firm that were great, but did I want to stop riding a skateboard for money? No. I also didn't like what was going on in the industry at the time. I hated the graphics and the advertising. I hated that Mike Vallely was the most popular skater one month, and then the next month there's an ad campaign saying his girlfriend is a slut, he's an idiot, and he sucks. I hated that stuff—it had nothing to do with skateboarding, it had to do with lame people finding a way to make a dollar, and it ruined skateboarding. The biggest reason I started the Firm was that there were no other companies out there that were what I thought skateboarding should be.

There was always vibing and likes and dislikes behind the scenes, but it became marketing in the early 1990s. It exposed the whole skate world to the slime that was unknown and behind the scenes, and everybody got drawn in, because it's such a small world. Then everybody was spreading the gossip and rumors, and it wasn't about skateboarding anymore. Brad Bowman doing an early-release air wasn't good enough anymore. Skateboarding wasn't interesting enough on its own, and I couldn't understand that, because I could look at Brad Bowman doing an early release and be totally inspired and want to go do it—but now the industry wasn't doing well, and something else had to come in to make more money. I understand why it went that way, but it was still a turd.

The major companies worked together through most of the '80s. Look what Stacy and [Craig] Stecyk and Fausto [*Vitello*] did with the early street skating. They saw what kids were doing and manipulated it and put it in magazines and created a healthy thing together as an industry. They didn't fight with one another.

One time Craig and Stacy took me down to *Transworld* to look at the magazine, and I realized that they all worked for rival companies. Stecyk worked for *Thrasher* and did Tracker ads. Stacy wrote for *Transworld* and was close with Fausto at Indy. They did it all for the good of skateboarding. I learned that you worked for skateboarding, and not for separate companies.

Today a lot of people just work for the companies, and that's eroded the industry. The big difference between skating back then and now is that there's a lot of money in it. A lot of current skating ads are focused on "Look what I've made from skate-boarding" and not "Look at it." Before, the focus in editorial or advertising was never about what [*material goods*] you can get from skateboarding.

It wasn't hard at all to put an end to the Firm in 2006. I never liked the way it made me feel. I'd stay up all night trying to figure it out. I'm a bum, not a business-man. Flip was the first company in fifteen years that thought I had more worth as a skateboarder than as a guy running a skateboard company. Now my only worry is if I'm going to get kicked off the team.

IRREPARABLE DAMAGE HAS BEEN DONE

Rodney Mullen: I never wanted to run a company. Absolutely not. I always had it in my mind that after skateboarding I was going back to school, probably the sciences. I really just wanted to do math. I got tricked into being involved with a company because my friend Steve [*Rocco*] had a lot of bad things happen to him. He was the team manager for Vision, and I don't know what the final straw was, but I know one time he stickered his boss's office with Powell Peralta stickers.

He showed up at my doorstep in Florida one evening. He'd driven 3,000 miles cross-country. He was pretty discombobulated and didn't know what to do. Six months or a year went by, it was 1987, and he said he was going to start a company called SMA Rocco Division. [*John*] Lucero bought in, then quickly came to his senses and bailed out.

Steve asked if I'd cut him a check and take Lucero's place. It was probably the low point for me with my family situation—I was out of the house and alone, and Steve came to me as my only real friend: "C'mon, Rodney, I could get other people to invest, but think about it—this could be us!"

I had saved a lot of money in the past, and my family had ended up losing it all. I had just started saving up again, and I thought, *I'm starting from ground zero as it is—what's the point? It can't be that bad even if he loses it—that's where I'm starting from anyway.* I assumed he'd lose it. I'll never forget handing him that $6,000 at LAX en route to a demo in Tahiti. I moved out to L.A. after that and skated and did whatever was needed at the company. There was nobody but Steve and me. I got to know the tape gun well. I did board shapes and even sales calls. Those started on a dare. I think the guy I called bought some boards only because he was stoked to talk to me, Rodney Mullen, the guy who had a pro model on Powell. Pretty soon George Powell called me and said, "Irreparable damage has been done."

I never looked at it as a real business. How stupid was I to get on the phone and call skate shops? Of course, George would call. Of course, that looks bad. But I didn't think it was a serious company—it was just me and Steve doing something as friends. I quit Powell shortly afterward.

We had no credit lines, and we lived and died by our cash flow. For a time, Steve's food budget was the money that kids sent in for stickers. Luckily, I still had demo income. And we had to have cash on hand to pay Suzuki [*a loan shark—name changed*].

It was scary. If we were short on a payment, Steve would leave the bag of cash with me and run out the back door. I was left to answer the questions. One time we had to borrow more money from Suzuki to pay off the interest due on his money. It was good in a way, because it created so much anxiety that you became numb to other stresses. Suzuki had an enforcer who we never saw, but we heard scary stories—people in hospitals on machines. If you saw that guy, it was already too late anyway. We actually became friends with Suzuki later. We have annual dinners together, and it's so much fun to talk about the old days.

I was surprised at the animosity from other skateboard companies and, later on, from some of the riders and ex-riders. Disgruntled skaters called me all kinds of things in public interviews because they felt I represented the business side of the company. It was very disorienting for me. Skateboarding was my life and everything I loved, and now I was involved with it in a different way. It really discombobulated me. My family experience wasn't that good, and so skateboarding filled that area in my life, and when I became a bad guy in the eyes of other skaters and companies, it was horrendous. It was traumatizing. Many, many times I thought of ways to get out of it. I went back and talked to my old professor in chemical research about getting a job.

Eventually we sold the company for $20 million. When we were talking to the bankers when we sold, they advised us to look authentic. Anything to help pass on the "charade" was good. One of the guys said, "Hey, smart move there" and pointed to the shoelace I was using as a belt. He thought it was part of a costume.

It took a long time, years and years, to get back to the point where I'm not very involved with companies and I can just skate. I still struggle with it here and there, but I'd be glad to turn down any amount of money not to be heavily involved in a skate company again. Not that it was so hellacious, but please don't put me through that again. It's difficult to walk that line between businessperson and skateboarder.

THE
AFTERLIFE

TEENAGE YEARS ARE PRIME FOR SKATING–YOUR BODY CAN TAKE THE ABUSE, AND YOU HAVE THE FREE TIME AND LACK OF RESPONSIBILITIES TO SHRED DAILY. But many hardcore skaters realize as they enter adulthood that they've inflicted irreparable damage, and not of the physical variety. The creativity that shaped their skating now shapes their adult lives, for better or worse.

Chris Haslam: I don't really know how skateboarding has affected my life because all I do right now is skate. I don't have a life without skating so I never really think about not skating. I don't have any other hobbies or anything.

I like being a part of something that not a lot of other people understand. It must look weird to somebody who doesn't know anything about skating to see us go up and start stroking a rail or a cement ledge. I love that feeling of being a skater, of seeing things differently than other people. The sense of community we have is like living in a really small town where everybody knows each other.

What would I do if I didn't skate? I used to play soccer all the time. I'd be a jock, a meathead, probably playing for a really horrible team.

Lance Mountain: What attracted me to skateboarding is different from what attracted Tony [Hawk] and Rodney [Mullen]. I think for them, the progression is a big part of what drives them. For me, it's the feeling that skateboarding gives. It's weird, because it's kind of part of the same thing.

It's like carving a pool, and you say, "I want to hit the tiles."

When you hit the tiles, then it's "I need to hit the top."

For me, it's a little bit less of wanting to hit the tiles for progression than Whoo!—that gave me a bit of a rush. I can get that rush forever, whereas Bob [Burnquist] jumps into the Grand Canyon. He actually told me, "I wish I could skate this every day."

I thought, What on earth are you talking about? This is a one-time stunt—it's a thrill.

But he wants to get that rush, which is at such a higher level for him. For me, hitting the tile is still fun.

This whole thing is a joke to me anyway—that we can skateboard on toys and have the possibility of not working. It's just a rad blessing to me.

Bob Burnquist: I try not to think about life after skating. Life after skating for me is when I die. I think about my body and health and try to get even stronger. I have special safety equipment like a body suit with custom padding on impact points.

Russ Howell: I don't really ever see myself stopping skating. It would feel too much like I was selling a piece of the farm, that I was diminishing myself. Skateboarding is such an individual activity that it leads to lifelong habits. It is a real connection back to my youth. Some of the locals here were learning older tricks, I mean really older tricks, and I re-learned a few of them. There was no difference in how I felt today compared to decades ago when I first learned them. But, obviously, in some ways skateboarding is different for me now than when I was in my twenties. Skateboarding was much more extroverted when I was doing demonstrations and contests and now it's introverted for me. But I still go out and do school demos and it's encouraging to be fifty-eight and have younger kids ask me how to skate.

Kevin Harris: The RDS indoor skatepark in Richmond, British Columbia, didn't work, and we had to close it in 2006. It's weird—there's this guy on the city council who I dealt with as a kid in the '70s, when I was trying to get a public skatepark built. He's still a councilman. I had the RDS park, and I wanted to donate the ramps to the city, so they could set up this world-class indoor skatepark. I left three messages with this guy, explaining how we had invested $800,000 in the park and wanted to *give* it to the city. The guy never returned a phone call. If that were a baseball field that I was donating, I'd get a call back that day. I'm forty-four years old now, and some things never change. I still feel like a ratty kid trying to talk to an adult and make him understand.

Jamie Thomas: Sometimes skating can be challenging, frustrating, or whatever, but in the end, it equates to what I associate with fun. Actually, I think fun is kind of a soft word for what skateboarding is. It's not really fun, it's good, great, terrible, worse—it's everything, all in one. Sometimes you hate the fact that you can't do certain tricks, and then you realize, *Whoa, it's not about the tricks. Let me take a step back.* And then ten minutes later, you love it. It's a schizophrenic relationship. It's always changing for me. When skating feels natural, when you just feel that you're supposed to be doing it at that time and place—that's the best feeling.

Stacy Peralta: Skating is liberating: You can just go outside your house and inter-pret it the way you want to. You can do it alone or with the best guy in the world. If you play basketball with the best guy in the world, he's going to kill you. And when you get on a court, you're confined to a rectangle and to one goal—to get that thing into the basket.

Skateboarding is not like that. You can turn your board, pop your board, go down, go up, go fast, go slow. Skateboarding teaches you to adapt, if you want to do it well. And adapting opens your mind to your own potential.

It's also illegal in a lot of places, which makes it really attractive. Everybody, deep down inside, wants to be a little rebellious, a little subversive. If you're riding a skatepark and some guy says, "Hey, there's a pool in a backyard two blocks away!" a lot of guys are going to leave that park to ride that pool, because there's just something really fun about that. It's an experience you can't get from a park—you only get it from sneaking into that backyard. I'm law-abiding, but it didn't keep me from sneaking into 200 backyards.

It changes your mind-set, because when you're expecting to get kicked out of everyplace, you have to outthink the people kicking you out. And you know what? It's really fun. The kids who stick with it, they celebrate that, whether they know it or not.

Daewon Song: I was a really angry kid. I fought every one of my friends in elemen-tary school. It was the weirdest thing. Skating made me a better person.

1

2

3

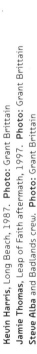

1 **Kevin Harris,** Long Beach, 1987. **Photo:** Grant Brittain
2 **Jamie Thomas,** Leap of Faith aftermath, 1997. **Photo:** Grant Brittain
3 **Steve Alba** and Badlands crew. **Photo:** Grant Brittain

Rodney Mullen: Throughout my life, skateboarding has been my life preserver. It's always been my constant. It's funny to even think that I'm forty and still skating. Skateboarding has given me an enthusiasm for just letting go of things. It's a freedom that skating has imbued me with, where you look at the world just a little different.

Mike Vallely: If you get into skateboarding with your antennae out and get the right information, it can be a life-changing experience. Showing that to kids is the role I want to play. Where else can a thirty-six-year-old have an on-the-level, real conversation with a twelve- or fourteen-year-old? A lot of people have proven that age doesn't really factor into skateboarding. If your limbs work and you're feeling it, than you can skate your ass off. I've seen plenty of guys older than me tearing much harder than me.

Jim Fitzpatrick: I don't know where creativity comes from or exactly what it is, but for me at least, it means you are thinking differently than normal people and skateboarding gave me that unique perspective. I stopped skating for practical reasons—I graduated and had a car and had a girl. It was like I was too old for skating in my mind. But then eight years later, in 1976, I kind of stole my neighbor's skateboard. He had a Sims with urethane wheels on his porch and I'd take it every day and ride it on the fresh blacktop at the local church and then put it back. I realized there had been this gap in my life and that skateboarding gave me that fresh youthful perspective. It's unbelievable how new and fresh skating is every single day.

Steve Olson: We skated pools and pipes—it's the same mission that I'm still on. Same as the street guys searching for rails. Going to ride a pool is the same exact deal: looking for a pool, trespassing, except you're forty-five and not fourteen.

I'm still the same person I was then. I'm totally into trying new shit and whatever. I love skateboarding now more than ever. I never stopped skating, even when the parks were down—there were always ditches and pools. Skating gave me a life. Skating is so excellent.

Tony Hawk: I thought thirty was when you had to be responsible and stop skating. I saw a picture with the caption "So-and-so is thirty and still going!" I thought, *Whoa, he's thirty and doing inverts!* He set the limit by default. But when I was thirty, I thought, *Are you kidding? I'm learning more tricks than ever.* I made the 900 when I was thirty-one.

The resurgence of vert helped because the ramps and equipment got better. I wasn't struggling with some rickety ramp. I started taking the terrain for granted and focused on what I wanted to do in the air. All of a sudden I could do all these tricks I always wanted to do like the 900, kickflip 540, varial 720, but never had the right circumstances when I was younger.

My body still worked the way it always had. My physical decline only happened when I broke my pelvis on the loop four years ago. I'm just now coming out of that injury and feel like I have a new lease.

Steve Alba: By the time I was seventeen, I had almost eighty grand in the bank. I blew it all after a while. I really regret that I could have bought my first house when I was seventeen for $28,000. I had the cash to do it right then and there. That was the biggest mistake of my life. But I skate because I love it—I've never skated for money.

Dave Hackett: The first time I saw anybody really do the loop was Tony Hawk in a bullfighting ring in Mexico in 1998. I thought, *That is so awesome—I have to do that someday*. And it didn't look that dangerous because I hadn't seen anybody slam on it yet. Later I heard that Tony built his own loop in Vista, California, but I didn't really know him and couldn't just call him up: "What's up? Can I come over and do the loop?" My days of being a top pro were long gone by the 1990s.

In August 2006, I got a call from [Steve] Olson, who's like my brother. "What are you doing? We're doing the loop!" He skates with Lance Mountain, and Tony told Lance the loop was set up.

I was scared, dude! I knew if I went over there, I'd try it. When Olson called, I was really looking for a way out. How am I going to tell my wife that I just broke my neck? That was a possibility. Tony fractured his pelvis and skull on that thing. It looks deceptively easy—when you make it. So Olson called me out, called me a pussy, and gave me directions. I didn't tell my wife.

Lance was dropping in from the take-off ramp, which is twenty-five feet high, and going all the way around into the gymnastic pads inside the loop. Olson was only running up the take-off ramp and doing a kickturn on the loop. He didn't want to drop in from the top. I thought, *Well, I can do that*. It was a total buddy-buddy deal. If those guys weren't there, there was no way I'd have tried it.

I ran up the take-off ramp, jumped on my board and kicked out of the loop at ten-thirty, flipped over and landed on my face on the bags. My board came down and speared me in the back. That was my first run.

[*Photographer Dan*] Sturt walked by and said, "You know, Hackett, if you do this, you'll be the oldest guy to do it."

I never think I'm forty-six. In my head, I'm nineteen. I said to Olson, "Let's just drop in from the top and see what happens."

I was seriously shacking. So what if there's a bag! I could still break my neck. I dropped in and went all the way around into the bag. I was on the bag thinking, *Woooow, that was sick! That felt bitchin'.*

I did it ten or fifteen more times before saying, "Let's just do this. Pull the bags." I just fucking went. I didn't even want to think about it.

When I came out the other end, I blew my own mind.

It's had a profound effect on me. I don't see boundaries any more. I had heard Tony say that as long as he's progressing, he's going to keep skating and I just now understand what he meant. It's changed my view of skateboarding.

Mike Vallely, Big in Japan, Tampa, 1995. **Photo:** Grant Brittain

Steve Olson, Runway banked slalom, 1980. **Photo:** James Cassimus

<u>Steve</u> <u>Olson</u>: If you can skate, you skate. Whatever.

ACKNOWLEDGMENTS

Sarah Malarkey, executive editor at Chronicle Books, scores
the acknowledgment crown for backing this little dirtbag book and
keeping it undiluted. Editor **Matt Robinson** also stepped in and
used his highly tuned Suck-O-Meter to detect and clear crap from
the manuscript. He also picked the title out of my sprawling list.
George Powell, **Bod Boyle**, and **James Cassimus** all graciously
helped with images. **Grant Brittain** not only set the standard
for modern skate photography, but he's an old friend who may be
the most sarcastic bastard in Southern California. He spent a Sunday
away from his family digging through his file cabinets of iconic
photos for this book. **All the skaters** I interviewed for *Stalefish*
have inspired me and deepened my appreciation for skating. I owe
all of them big time. I'm thinking of starting a fan club for each of
them. My **family** and **friends**...umm, thanks for being my family
and friends. And lastly, thanks to **Stacy Peralta** who advised
me to try writing way back in 1989.